THE SHORT & CURLY GUIDE TO LIFE

PUFFIN BOOKS

PUFFIN BOOKS

UK | USA | Canada | Ireland | Australia
India | New Zealand | South Africa | China

Penguin Books is part of the Penguin Random House group
of companies whose addresses can be found at global.penguinrandomhouse.com.

First published by Penguin Random House Australia Pty Ltd, 2018

Text copyright © Australian Broadcasting Corporation 2018
Illustrations copyright © Simon Greiner 2018

The ABC logo is a registered trademark of the Australian Broadcasting Corporation
and is used under licence by Penguin Random House Australia.

The moral right of the author has been asserted.

All rights reserved. Without limiting the rights under copyright reserved above, no part of this
publication may be reproduced, stored in or introduced into a retrieval system, or transmitted, in
any form or by any means (electronic, mechanical, photocopying, recording or otherwise), without
the prior written permission of both the copyright owner and the above publisher of this book.

 A catalogue record for this
book is available from the
National Library of Australia

ISBN: 978 0 14379 218 5

Cover and internal design by Rachel Lawston
Illustrations by Simon Greiner
Printed in China

penguin.com.au

THE SHORT & CURLY GUIDE TO LIFE

WRITTEN BY **DR MATT BEARD**
AND **KYLA SLAVEN**

ILLUSTRATED BY SIMON GREINER

PUFFIN BOOKS

CONTENTS

Introducing Short & Curly 6

Lying 18

Happiness 30

Learning 46

Life Choices 60

Letting Go 74

Fairness 88

Trends 102

Promises 114

Friendship 128

Bravery 142

Fighting 154

Integrity 168

Final Philoso-mail 184

The Short & Curly Podcast 187

INTRODUCING SHORT & CURLY

PSST! HEY, YOU!

Yeah, you. The one reading this. Pay attention for a second!

It's your lucky day! You're about to join a crack team of super-clever, elite, brave, ridiculously good-looking and fun researchers. That's right, you're now joining team Short & Curly.

What's Short & Curly? If you've never heard of us, you're in for a treat.

Short & Curly is a podcast made by the ABC. It asks short and tricky (curly) questions about the world around us. Why are things the way they are? Why do we do things a certain way? Wouldn't it be better if we did things differently?

It's all about **ethics** – more on that later.

First, there is something important you need to know about Short & Curly. Not only are we a totally awesome podcast, we are also an extremely elaborate, complicated and very cool research program. We send our team of researchers, AKA the **BRAINS TRUST**, out into the world to find the trickiest situations, the thorniest questions and the toughest topics for us to discuss, explore and learn how to make good decisions. Our Brains Trust team find questions anywhere and everywhere.

The world of Short & Curly is topsy-turvy. One moment we'll be talking about the stuff that happens in your classroom at school, the next we might be flying to Mars! You'll find strangeness in the most ordinary things, and find something familiar in situations beyond your wildest imagination. So get ready: in Short & Curly, there's no saying what might happen next. ROBOTS might attack while you're doing your homework . . . or they might not. Which means you'll have to find another excuse for not handing in your maths on time.

Basically, we don't like the word 'normal' here. 'Normal' is a boring word. And at Short & Curly, we don't do boring.

Oh, one last thing. While you read this book, you might come up with research ideas, questions or thoughts of your own. If you do, make sure you don't forget them. At the back of the book, you'll find an email address where you can send us your own questions, discoveries or ideas (just get one of the adults in your life to give you the OK first). Never let a good question go to waste!

WHAT ON EARTH IS ETHICS?

I told you before that Short & Curly is all about ethics. So what on earth is ethics?

Well, ethics is part of **philosophy**, and philosophy asks big questions about the nature of things, and tries to answer those questions in an organised way. It encourages us to think differently, ask tough questions and to be OK when the answers aren't black and white.

Ethics is a kind of philosophy. It's the word we use when philosophers ask questions about good, bad, right and wrong. Whenever we ask 'what should I do?' we're doing ethics.

This is important: we are doing ethics when we ask questions and try to think through the answers for ourselves. It's not about thinking what other people want us to think or doing what other people tell us to do, it's about finding our own answers and testing what we (and others) think is right.

So whenever someone says 'everybody does it this way', 'that's the way it's always been done', or 'do it because I said so', it's ethics-o-clock. Every time we make a choice, we change the world a little bit. Ethics is about working out what kind of world we should try to create and live in. Which takes a lot of imagination. You can't change the world unless you can imagine a different one!

Before we get started you should know: doing ethics comes with a VERY SERIOUS, EXTREMELY IMPORTANT and VERY BIG WRITTEN WARNING!

BE PREPARED TO NEVER SEE THE WORLD IN THE SAME WAY AGAIN

Oh, and one more warning: ethics field research can be DANGEROUS. A long time ago, in ancient Greece, a man named **Socrates** was told he was the wisest person in all of Greece. This was a weird thing for Socrates to hear, because he was pretty sure he didn't know anything! How could he be the wisest if he didn't know anything?

Socrates thought about this for a while and decided the only way he could be the wisest is because *nobody* knows anything. See, everyone else thought they knew heaps of stuff, but they were wrong. Socrates didn't think he knew anything, and he was right! So that's what made him the wisest.

Having worked this out, Socrates decided to become history's first ethics field researcher. He chatted to all kinds of people who thought they knew stuff. He would keep asking them questions and get them to explain what they knew until in the end, they realised they didn't know anything at all. This was so annoying that eventually the leaders of Athens sentenced Socrates to death.

Even though it was a pretty grizzly end for our pal Socrates, he lived what philosophers would think was a really good life: asking lots of hard questions, trying to understand the world around him and being brave in seeking the truth. And that's exactly what we're going to do.

MEET MATT!

Locked away, in a dark dungeon in the heart of Short & Curly HQ lives a man nerdier and more curious and obsessed with ethics than anyone you could ever imagine. His job at Short & Curly is to help people examine the prickly questions the Brains Trust uncover during their research. He is Short & Curly's philosopher-in-chief, and his name is Dr Matt Beard.

And he's me! Hello!

Also, I'm not really locked in a dungeon. My office has lots of windows, but I am sometimes trapped inside because I pile all my books up at the door. I usually find my way out in time for dinner.

I'm a philosopher, and even though I'm not as famous as Socrates, we're both members of the same club. As a philosopher, I take our everyday beliefs about how the world works and look at them very closely. I want to understand exactly what people mean when they tell me what they think, and I want to know if what they think is true. I like to ask questions that turn our world upside down. That helps me take a good look at what's really going on and gives my imagination a solid workout.

But I'm not *just* a philosopher. I have other hobbies too! I LOVE ice cream, pizza, garlic bread, hot chips and lemon chicken. And I find it sad that I can't eat them all day long. I like singing and playing the piano, even though I'm bad at it. I love making puns and I get super, over-the-top excited about anything to do with fantasy, science fiction or comic books.

Enough about me though – let's get down to the nitty-gritty. It's my job to guide you through the different adventures you're going to read from our talented and dedicated Brains Trust agents. They have been out in the wild and reported back on some seriously 'curly' situations – and you're lucky enough to get to read their final reports! With every case I'll be there along the way, talking through different ideas and asking some tricky questions.

Remember, philosophy and ethics are great to do as a team! I'll give you questions that are fun to discuss with your classmates, friends, family or whoever is nearby when you're reading this book. You can always put the book down for a while to speak to someone and see what they have to say. Not everything we talk about has a clear 'right' and 'wrong' answer, so it's good to chat with a whole bunch of people and see what they think.

MEET THE BRAINS TRUST

Now to introduce the **Brains Trust** – our team of young researchers who we send out into the world to watch people going about their lives and trying to solve the ethical dilemmas that face them. They take notes, make observations and send their toughest, curliest questions back to our philosopher-in-chief, Dr Matt Beard (that's me, remember!). Our Brains Trust is full of imaginative, curious, brave and quirky young people. And here they are!

AGENT ARJUN

At just 11 years old, Arjun knows anything and everything about sport. He can tell you who won the Olympic gold medal for javelin in 2000 and which football team has won the most matches this season.

When he's not out in the field studying ethics, you can usually find Arjun on either a basketball or tennis court. He wants to go professional! He thinks sportsmanship is really important, and would rather lose playing with a good spirit than win by breaking the rules.

You can always spot one of Arjun's research reports because he takes note of any food he can see. Arjun is *always* hungry – as soon as he gets back to Short & Curly HQ, he raids the fridge for a feast before shooting some hoops out the back.

AGENT RABIA

Rabia is the most curious ten-year-old you'll ever meet. She's perfect for the Brains Trust because she has so many curly questions she wants to discuss. She is always trying to find out how things work by reading, doing experiments and spending lots of time in nature. When she grows up she wants to be a scientist – but really, she's already a pretty great scientist!

Rabia is also a total movie buff. She loves all kinds of movies: cartoons, comedies, action, even horror! (At least, the ones her parents let her watch.) Rabia's field research usually has a bunch of movie references in it. She just can't help it. She thinks movies are an effective way to think and learn about ethics – and to be honest, she's right.

AGENT KOA

Koa is the oldest and wisest member of our Brains Trust. He's 12, and is Short & Curly's creative cat! He's into all things art. He likes sketching, painting and has recently started learning how to do graphic design on computers. Koa has a lot of fun putting his friends' faces onto movie posters to make it look like they're famous actors!

Don't ever try to hog the video game controller when Koa's around. He LOVES video games, and he's pretty good at them too. Puzzle-solving games are his favourite, but he'll play just about anything.

Koa enjoys telling stories. His research reports often include little stories from his own life that relate to what he's observing. It's a great way for him to feel a close connection to the ethical problems he's thinking about, which makes him an important member of our Brains Trust.

AGENT SOPHIA

Sophia is the youngest member of our Brains Trust. She's nine, and if Short & Curly HQ had a zoo, Sophia would be the zookeeper. She is a genius when it comes to taking care of animals. It doesn't matter if your animal is cute and cuddly, slimy, scaly or scary, Sophia loves them all. She's even got a pet lizard (called Liz) who she takes everywhere – even out on research missions!

Sophia's research reports are sometimes a bit hard to read because she's easily distracted. Often she'll be halfway through a thought and then forget what she was doing! But she always gets there in the end. Plus, 'Sophia' is the ancient Greek word for 'Wisdom', so how could we not have her in the Brains Trust?

AGENT MAE

Mae is the cheekiest 11-year-old you'll ever meet. You can't let your guard down when Mae is about. She thinks she's a ninja and is always sneaking around trying to surprise unsuspecting victims! Mae likes being part of the Brains Trust because observing people out in the real world lets her practise her stealth skills.

Mae also loves making bad jokes. If she doesn't become a ninja, she's planning on becoming a comedian. That might be tricky, because even though Mae LOVES jokes, they're all pretty lame. Still, Mae keeps everybody laughing – and on our toes – which is important, because to do ethics well, you need to be agile!

ETHICAL TOOLKIT

Throughout our adventures together, we're going to use a few different tools to work out whether something is good or bad, right or wrong, allowed or not allowed . . . you get the picture. Think of them like a bunch of tools in an explorer's backpack. Flick back to this page if you need a bit more information when you come across one of these terms in the book.

A MAP

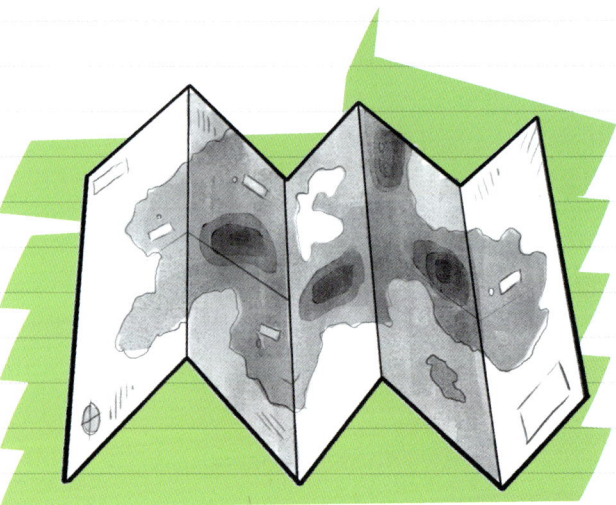

This helps us to see the big picture, even in strange places. When explorers want to know how to get somewhere they've never been before, they use a map. When philosophers want to understand an idea they haven't come across before, they use a **thought experiment**.

Thought experiments work a bit like science experiments. When scientists have an idea they want to test, what do they do? They create an experiment to test it out in a lab. Philosophers sometimes do the same thing, but we use a different kind of lab – one in the gooey grey matter of our brains. We create imaginary situations and think about what we would think or do in these weird scenarios. We don't just do it because it's fun (it is sometimes), we do it to test some of our ideas.

Thought experiments help us work out what is important in real life, even when we're in strange or unfamiliar situations. You know what else does that? You guessed it: a map.

A TORCH

This helps us spot things that are hard to notice. Lots of the trickiest ethical situations happen when we're dealing with things we can't know for sure or can't see clearly. And you know what the hardest thing is to see clearly? What's going on in someone else's head!

Sometimes figuring out what to do requires us to understand what someone is thinking, how they are feeling and what they care about.

Other people's minds are similar to dark caves. We can't ever see everything in there. We might be able to see a little bit, and guess which way the exit is, but we'll never see it in full. That's why we need a tool like a torch, to guide us through the spooky darkness of other people's heads. And in ethics, we have two torches that help us do this: **curiosity and empathy**.

A MACHETE

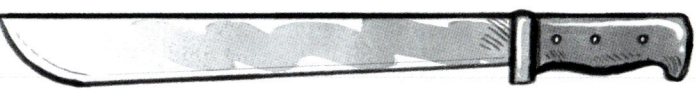

The perfect tool for **making distinctions**, which is a useful way to figure out why things that seem similar on the surface are actually different. We can get really confused if we assume things are the same when they're different in important ways. So we use our **machetes** to slice things apart and spot the difference.

COMPASS

This awesome tool ensures we stay on the right track. Even in confusing, complex terrain you can look down at your compass and make sure you're not straying off course.

In ethics, we want to make sure our thinking stays on track too. This means you need to check yo'self!

15

We call this **checking assumptions**, and it's really important. When we don't know something, our brains try to fill in the blanks with guesses, but lots of the time we get it wrong. That's why it's essential to check what we think we know and make sure we have good reasons for thinking the way we do, because we might be wrong.

BINOCULARS

These are perfect for spotting things we might have missed. When we're doing field research, it's easy to get so focused on what's right in front of us that we forget to see the big picture. That's what binoculars are for! We can see the stuff on the horizon we might not have noticed or thought of yet. Here at Short & Curly we make sure we're always **fact finding** to make sure we've got all the information we need to make the best decision.

A MAGNIFYING GLASS

The ideal instrument for being precise. Remember how we said in ethics we try to give organised answers to tough questions? That means we need to be very detailed in the way we use words. Just like researchers use a magnifying glass to look at things up close, we do the same when we want to **define our terms** and spell out what we mean when we use certain words.

HIKING POLES

In order to keep ourselves balanced we need these trusty tools. Sometimes we can't rely on our own two feet. We need something to lean on – like **hiking poles**.

When we're doing ethics, it's the same. If we're stressed, excited, anxious or any of the other hundred emotions we might be feeling, we can easily get caught up and use our feelings to help decide what's right and what's wrong. We use our hearts instead of our heads; we assume if something makes us happy, is funny or makes us feel safe, it's good and if it makes us angry, sad or feel gross, then it's bad. That's not always a good way to make decisions, which is why in ethics we try to **question our emotions**. Our head and heart both matter, but we need to make sure we don't lose our head when things get a bit wild!

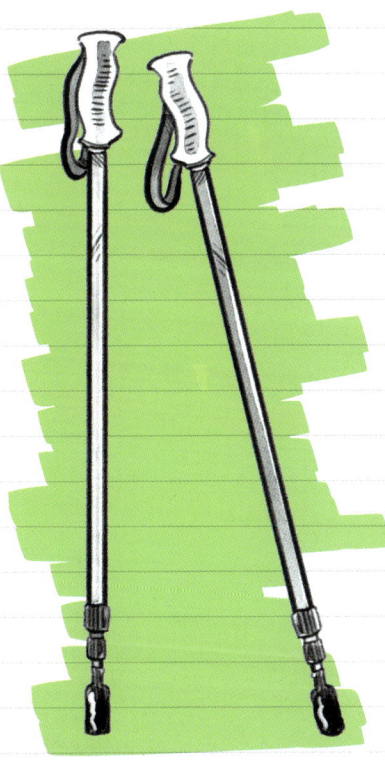

AND THAT'S IT! KEEP AN EYE OUT FOR LITTLE REMINDERS TO USE THESE TOOLS THROUGHOUT YOUR RESEARCH MISSIONS. GOOD LUCK OUT THERE!

THE DOG THAT'S NOT A DOG

FIELD RESEARCH REPORT:

SUBJECT: Alinta Orkins

DETAILS: Bought an adorable new Shiba Inu puppy, but she might be in for a surprise.

NOTES:

- Is it OK to tell a lie to make someone feel better?
- When do you have to tell the truth?
- Are we sometimes better off not knowing the truth?

REPORT RUN-DOWN

NEW MESSAGE

TO: DR MATT @ SHORT & CURLY HQ
FROM: AGENT SOPHIA @ BRAINS TRUST
SUBJECT: REPORT RUN-DOWN ON ALINTA ORKINS

We received word that someone nearby had purchased an ADORABLE new puppy. It's a Shiba Inu. Have you seen them? They're SO cute! There's no big ethical problem here, but I couldn't resist. I just had to sneak out and watch the nugget racing around the backyard and playing with his new owner, Alinta.

Alinta is super nice and really excited about her new pet. She's been saving up her pocket money for a whole year to buy Shibastian (get it? Sebastian, but a Shiba?). She was so lucky — she saw an ad online just yesterday. A breeder had ONE PUPPY LEFT and had to sell it by the end of the day because they were moving to another state. The breeder was also happy to take less money, which was great because Alinta didn't have enough to buy a Shiba at full price. It still cost her all her savings, but it's totally worth it for a cute little Shiba, right?

That's what I thought, until I saw Shibastian. He's not a Shiba at all. He's a **FOX!**

Alinta got ripped off! I bet the breeder has already disappeared with her money. Oh no! She's going to be so upset and embarrassed when she learns the truth. Plus, foxes aren't domesticated animals. There's a good chance Shibastian the Fox is going to get pretty mean and aggressive as he gets older.

I overheard Alinta's parents having a conversation about what to do with this new furry friend.

DAD: That Shiba looks... I don't know. A bit strange. I wish Alinta had told us before she bought it, I would have come along and asked the breeder some questions.

MUM: Breeder? Come on – it's obvious. That's not a Shiba, it's a fox! What breeder doesn't give a breeding certificate, a contact number in case anything goes wrong or even an address? Our little girl has been ripped off. I've called my brother. He's coming over later today.

DAD: You mean Trevor? Trevor fixes cars for a living – what's he going to do to help?

MUM: Not Trevor, you dork! Neville – he's a vet, remember!

DAD: Oh right. Yeah, he might be more useful.

MUM: We're going to have to tell Alinta that she's been tricked and Neville can get rid of the fox. We'll just have to buy her a new puppy to make her feel better. This is kind of our fault anyway – we should have gone with her.

DAD: But she'll be so upset! The fox isn't going to be any trouble until it's bigger. Can't she just be happy and play with it for a while? Then we can deal with it later.

MUM: So what, you want us to lie and say it's an adorable puppy?

DAD: Maybe. I just don't want to hurt her feelings.

WHAT SHOULD ALINTA'S PARENTS DO? SHOULD THEY TELL A LIE – JUST FOR A LITTLE WHILE – TO PROTECT HER FEELINGS? OR SHOULD THEY TELL THE TRUTH, EVEN IF IT BREAKS HER HEART? ARE ALL LIES BAD?

Agent Sophia signing out

INCOMING PHILOSO-MAIL

NEW MESSAGE

TO: AGENT SOPHIA @ BRAINS TRUST
FROM: DR MATT @ SHORT & CURLY HQ
SUBJECT: DR MATT PHILOSO-MAIL

I don't know what the saddest part of this story is: a little fox without its mum, Alinta being lied to and ripped off, or the fact she's wasted the *brilliant* name Shibastian on a fox!

Also, it's lucky you've managed to stumble on some ethics after sneaking out of Short & Curly HQ to go look at cute puppies. How dare you leave without inviting the rest of us?!

Anyway, let's get back to your question. To start with, why are lies bad? We're always told they are, but why?

The reason people tend to say lying is bad is because we think there's something very special about knowing what's true. Knowing stuff is wonderful. Understanding the world around us is only possible because we can *know* the world as it really is. Lies destroy this knowledge. They pretend something is true when it isn't.

Lies are also bad for our freedom. Most people think it's important for people to make decisions for themselves – it's what puts us in the driver's seat of our own lives. When we're lied to, we can't be in control because we don't have the right information to make good decisions.

This is why people tend to think lying is a problem. But not all lies are the same. We need to get our **machete** out to slice up some **distinctions**. There are lots of different kinds of lies, and it's worth knowing the difference.

1. Selfish lies to help ourselves: Sometimes we lie to get an advantage over other people. The fake Shiba breeder told Alinta a lie so he could make some easy money. He's just in it for himself and he's willing to trick other people.

2. Selfish lies to protect ourselves: There are lies we tell to stop ourselves from getting in trouble. For example, you've been told 20 times not to play cricket in the house, but you do it anyway. You smash the ball and it goes right into Mum's precious vase. It's a family heirloom and now it's shattered. You might lie and tell your mum the cat did it to stop yourself from getting into trouble. That's still selfish, but in a slightly different way.

3. Lies to protect someone's feelings: Someone asks you what you think of their new haircut. You think they look pretty scary, but you don't want to hurt their feelings. You could lie and say they look great. They'll feel better about themselves and you won't seem like a nasty person.

4. Lies to stop something bad happening: You hear a knock at the door. It's a scary man with an axe! He very politely asks where your brother is because he'd like to chop off a couple of his toes. You know your brother is upstairs. Do you tell the truth? Or tell a lie to keep him safe?

The selfish lies seem worse because they come from bad intentions. You're not helping anyone, you're using other people to get what you want.

The other lies are trying to protect people or stop them from being hurt. This might seem like the kindest thing to do, but does that make it OK? Maybe. But we need to remember: when we lie, we take ownership of the situation because we're the only ones with all the knowledge. That means we need to accept a lot of the responsibility for what happens after we lie.

Let's imagine Alinta's parents tell her the truth about Shibastian. They could go to the police and try to catch the fake dog breeder. However, if they lie, they'd have to take responsibility for potentially letting that sly fox get away.

Dr Matt signing out

THINKING QUESTIONS

1. Do you think it's ever OK to tell a lie?

2. If someone told a lie to protect your feelings, and later you found out they'd lied to you, how would you feel?

3. If you were Alinta's parents, what would you do?

SLOW DOWN, FIBBER!

In 2012, three researchers named **Shaul Shalvi**, **Ori Eldar** and **Yoella Bereby-Meyer** published a study looking at what helps people to tell the truth.

They found out a bunch of different things, but one of the most interesting ones was that people are more likely to lie if they're in a rush. When people have time to think about things and plan *how* they'd tell the truth in a nice way, they're less likely to lie. When we're put on the spot, we're more likely to tell a porky.

If you're tempted to tell a fib, it's a good idea to take five minutes and ask yourself, 'If I was going to tell the truth, what would I say?' Think of the best way to make your point. Then compare the 'best version' of the truth to your lie. Chances are, the truth is going to look like a better option most of the time.

SORRY! GOTTA RUN! IT'S MY MONKEY'S BIRTHDAY!

RESEARCH UPDATE

NEW MESSAGE

TO: DR MATT @ SHORT & CURLY HQ
FROM: AGENT SOPHIA @ BRAINS TRUST
SUBJECT: RESEARCH UPDATE ON ALINTA ORKINS

OK, Uncle Nev arrived and told Alinta's mum and dad that Shibastian is definitely a fox. They've decided to tell Alinta the truth: that she's been tricked, foxes can be dangerous and they'll have to take Shibastian away and buy a new puppy later.

The thing is, when they told Alinta, she wouldn't change her mind! She said she didn't care and that she loves Shibastian. She said she's going to care for him and she knows he'll never hurt her because she's going to love him so much.

'I paid for him, he's my pet and I don't want you to take him away!'

Uncle Nev pointed out that it's illegal to keep foxes as pets. Oh no! Are the police going to come and put Shibastian in tiny, adorable handcuffs?

Nev also said foxes are dangerous to other pets. Shibastian might hurt some of the other dogs and cats in the neighbourhood. Alinta wasn't interested. It looks like she loves the little fella and believes she can help him to be well-behaved.

The argument was going nowhere, so Nev and Alinta's parents went into the kitchen for a little chat while Alinta taught Shibastian to jump through a hula hoop (he's doing it!).

Nev came up with a plan. He's going to come back late at night when Alinta's asleep and collect Shibastian. He'll take him to a wildlife park where he knows they will take good care of him. In the morning, they'll tell Alinta the fox ran away and then later, when she's got a new puppy and she's really happy, they'll tell her the truth – Shibastian is at a wildlife park where she can visit him whenever she likes.

What a perfect solution. Clever Uncle Nev! Guess there are no more ethical pickles here. See you back at HQ!

Agent Sophia signing out

INCOMING PHILOSO-MAIL

NEW MESSAGE

TO: AGENT SOPHIA @ BRAINS TRUST
FROM: DR MATT @ SHORT & CURLY HQ
SUBJECT: DR MATT PHILOSO-MAIL

Stay right where you are! There's plenty of ethics still to talk about here!

Uncle Nev's solution is very creative and it ticks a lot of boxes, but that doesn't mean it's completely ethical. After all, they're still lying to Alinta.

Some ethicists won't think this is a problem because the outcome is a good one in the end. These people are called **consequentialists**. That's a fancy name for people who think good actions are ones that lead to good outcomes. They think it's OK to tell a lie for the greater good. A consequentialist would think Uncle Nev's plan is a great example of a 'good lie'.

However, not everyone is a consequentialist. Some people think lies are just *bad*, not because of their outcomes, but because they are disrespectful to the person being lied to. For these people, Uncle Nev's clever plan is no better than any other lie.

Here's one thing to think about: right now, it seems pretty clear that Alinta can't have a pet fox. It's illegal, unsafe and unfair on all the other pets in the area. But if we get our **torches** out and practise some **curiosity and empathy**, it's pretty easy to understand why she can't see it that way. She loves Shibastian!

If Alinta is given some time to think about it, she has the chance to do the right thing. She can make a choice to keep everyone safe, but that choice is being taken away from her. Alinta is being *forced* to do the right thing when, with a bit of time, she might work it out for herself!

She might even find the decision easier if she knew Shibastian could live happily in a wildlife park where foxes get to have massages all day, lie by the pool and play beach volleyball. The point is, if Alinta had all the facts, she might be OK with Uncle Nev's solution. So why not include her? Remember, our **binoculars** are important because it's hard to make the right decision without all the relevant information. And right now, Alinta needs some more information that isn't being given to her.

Even though Uncle Nev's plan is a good one and will get the best outcome, is it the right way to get the best result?

Dr Matt signing out

THINKING QUESTIONS

1. Is it OK to tell a lie so long as you tell the truth later? Can you think of any examples from your own life?

2. If you were Alinta, how would you feel about being lied to? Would it matter if you found out Shibastian would be OK after you'd already given him up?

RIDDLE ME THIS!

Here's a famous riddle all about lying and telling the truth!

You're in a room with two doors. In front of each door is a tough-looking guard. They both look exactly the same. One door leads to the exit, the other door leads to a giant, hungry dragon that will eat you. But you don't know which door is which.

You're allowed to ask *one* question to *one* of the guards to work out which door to go through. Problem is, there's a catch: one of the guards *always tells lies* and one of the guards *always tells the truth.*

And you don't know which guard is honest and which is the liar!

What is the one question you could ask which would make the guards tell you which door is safe, even though you don't know if they're telling the truth or lying?

SOLUTION

Ask either guard which door the other guard would say is the safe exit, then choose the opposite door.

If you ask the honest guard, he'll direct you to the deadly door (because the lying guard will fib). So you should pick the opposite door.

If you ask the lying guard, he'll lie and direct you to the deadly door (because the honest guard would point you to the exit), so you should pick the opposite door.

Tricky, huh?

AGENT DEBRIEF

NEW MESSAGE
TO: DR MATT @ SHORT & CURLY HQ
FROM: AGENT SOPHIA @ BRAINS TRUST
SUBJECT: AGENT SOPHIA – DEBRIEF FOR HQ

When Uncle Nev first came up with his plan to help Alinta's family fib their way out of a foxy situation I thought it was a great idea. After all, it gets the job done, it's good for the neighbourhood pets and makes sure Alinta doesn't get into trouble for raising a fox! Plus, Shibastian goes to a caring home. To be honest, the fib still seems like a good idea in the grand scheme of things.

However, when I think about it from Alinta's perspective, everything changes. The lie treats Alinta like she's not smart enough to make the right decision for herself. Her parents and Uncle Nev are assuming she won't listen to reason (and to be fair, she didn't the first time they chatted) and so they think they have to lie to get the job done. I can see how that would leave Alinta feeling pretty down and hurt.

Still, what's more important? The truth and Alinta's feelings or doing what needs to be done? That's a tough one . . . I'll think about it on the way back to HQ. But first, I heard there's a new baby wombat at the zoo. I DEFINITELY think it's going to cause some important ethical issues – I'm absolutely NOT skipping out of work to look at cute animals.

Or am I lying . . . ?

Agent Sophia signing out

PLUGGING INTO HAPPILY EVER AFTER

FIELD RESEARCH REPORT:

SUBJECT: Sam Eton

DETAILS: Superhero, rock star, all-round cool dude.

NOTES:

- Is infinite happiness possible?
- Would it be wrong to do whatever made us happy, no matter what?

REPORT RUN-DOWN

NEW MESSAGE

TO: DR MATT @ SHORT & CURLY HQ
FROM: AGENT MAE @ BRAINS TRUST
SUBJECT: REPORT RUN-DOWN ON SAM ETON

Sam Eton is a superhero. He can fly, has super strength and can become invisible when he wants! He's also a rock star in his spare time. His band, The Supersams, are probably the most popular band in the world – and he's the lead singer. Sam's got it all – he's funny, smart and has a talking pet dog. It's hard to imagine anybody who wouldn't be jealous of Sam!

Except Sam isn't actually a superhero. He's just an ordinary boy, with a rather extraordinary toy. He has a special room in his house that lets him do something incredible. Just past the laundry there's a teensy-weensy room with a single chair, a set of goggles and a big, fancy machine with lots of shiny buttons that makes a slow, humming noise.

When Sam puts on the goggles, he enters a virtual reality where he can do whatever he wants. His parents – the ones who built the room – are genius scientists. They research ways to help make people happier, and their latest idea looks like it'll be a major breakthrough. They call it 'Happily Ever After'. (It's a bit cheesy, I know. I'd call it the 'Smile-ulator' – like simulator, but with smiles, get it?)

Happily Ever After is designed to make you as happy as you can ever be. Before you go into the machine, you answer hundreds of questions about yourself. The machine uses those questions to design your perfect reality. Then all you have to do is plug into the machine and you'll be able to live your best life without doing anything to get it! Amazing, right?

There's a problem though. Every time Sam leaves Happily Ever After, he finds himself more and more annoyed and frustrated with the real world. When he's not in the machine, he can't fly or lift cars, he's not a good singer and his dog just barks at him.

Tonight, Sam was having dinner with his parents (cauliflower soup – blergh). They told him they've come up with a solution to his woes: Sam could plug into the machine forever. No more disappointment when Sam unplugs, just superheroes and rock shows all day, every day.

Of course, Sam's parents would never be able to talk to him again, and they'd miss him terribly, but they just want him to be happy – and this is the best way to make that happen. Sam won't miss his mum and dad because he'll have a digital version of them in Happily Ever After. Plus, they'll be better versions of his parents. They won't get sick or grumpy, they'll always cook his favourite foods and won't dance like dorks around the kitchen while his friends are visiting, which Sam finds SOOOO embarrassing!

IT SOUNDS PRETTY GOOD, BUT SAM ISN'T SURE. SHOULD HE PLUG INTO THE MACHINE FOREVER? CAN A MACHINE REALLY MAKE US HAPPY?

Agent Mae signing out

INCOMING PHILOSO-MAIL

NEW MESSAGE
TO: AGENT MAE @ BRAINS TRUST
FROM: DR MATT @ SHORT & CURLY HQ
SUBJECT: DR MATT PHILOSO-MAIL

I wonder what kind of world Happily Ever After would invent for me . . . I bet I'd be able to eat pizza, hot chips and ice cream every day without ever getting sick or unhealthy. I'd be able to memorise every book I read and I'd be the smartest, funniest person in town. I mean, not that I'm not already the smartest, funniest person around . . .

Anyway, back to Sam. Before he plugs in for good, he might want to take a closer look at what's at stake. Is his life in Happily Ever After going to be 'happy' or just pleasurable? If he stays in the real world, will it be painful or will he suffer?

That means he's gonna have to whip out his handy-dandy **magnifying glass** to **define some terms.** In this case, we need to define a bunch of different feelings that sometimes get confused for one another.

- **Pleasure** is any good feeling. These feelings are usually pretty quick and then they vanish. Eating ice cream is pleasurable (and if you don't think so, you're wrong), it makes you feel good until it runs out. Then, if you're like me, you'll feel sad and go looking for more ice cream. Then you'll eat it until you feel sick. And when you feel sick, you'll be in pain.

- **Pain** is the opposite of pleasure – it refers to any bad feeling. Some pain (like pleasure) is physical, which means it makes our bodies feel bad. Other pains can be emotional – like feeling sad, anxious, bored or angry. Most kinds of pain, like pleasures, don't last very long.

- **Happiness** is living a life that you're generally pretty satisfied with. It's a lot more than just pleasure. When we talk about wanting the people we love to be happy, we don't mean we want them to walk around smiling like idiots all the time! For some people, pleasure might be enough to make them happy. Most people need more. They want to feel like they're living their dreams and doing things that matter. They want to have good relationships and be respected by the people around them. This means making someone happy is harder than simply giving them lots of ice cream (except for me – I just want the ice cream, thanks).

- **Suffering** is when we experience something so bad it makes it difficult to be happy. Some pain can be a kind of suffering, but there are other kinds of suffering which don't cause pain. Loneliness, feeling like a failure or losing someone close to you can all be kinds of suffering. Suffering is usually long-lasting and gets in the way of our ability to live a good, happy life. That makes it a more serious issue than pain.

If Sam plugs into the machine, he's definitely going to feel lots of pleasure and not feel any pain. But will that make him happy? Remember, not all pain is bad. Sometimes, we feel pain because we've been working hard to master a new skill or saving up for something we want. In these cases, the pain might actually make us feel *more* happiness when the time comes.

Happiness is partly about living our dreams, and most of the time our dreams get bigger the more we struggle for them. If Sam never has to struggle, he'll have a lot of fun, but it's not clear whether that fun will make him happy.

Dr Matt signing out

QUICK NOTE:

Pleasure and pain aren't special, ethically speaking. Some pleasure is good and some pleasure is bad. Some pain is good and some is bad. You might get a lot of pleasure from watching a bus drive through a deep puddle and soak a little old lady walking home from the shops. That doesn't mean it was good she got soaked. You might also feel some pain if you stick up for a friend who is being bullied, but that doesn't mean it was bad to stick up for your friend.

THE NEW YEAR'S EVE EFFECT

New Year's Eve is an emotional roller-coaster. Everyone wants to have the BEST PARTY EVER. They expect it to be a ridiculously fun night where they can ride dragons, surf on clouds and dance on water – OK, maybe that's just me. The big expectations around New Year's Eve actually make it pretty disappointing in the end.

A bunch of researchers studied people who had made plans to party until the fireworks popped and they found almost everyone was disappointed. They didn't have as much fun as they thought they would. Even more surprising, the people who expected to have the most fun were the most disappointed! Funny, huh?

It turns out, when your expectations for happiness are too high, you tend not to enjoy what you're doing as much. That makes it hard to build a machine *guaranteed* to make us happy, doesn't it?

Can you think of something you were really looking forward to – something you thought was going to be *the best thing ever* that wasn't as good as you thought?

RESEARCH UPDATE

NEW MESSAGE
TO: DR MATT @ SHORT & CURLY HQ
FROM: AGENT MAE @ BRAINS TRUST
SUBJECT: RESEARCH UPDATE ON SAM ETON

I have a research update boss, but I have to admit, I did something an itty-bitty bit unethical to get this new information. After Sam had spoken with his parents, he spent a long time in his room thinking and writing in his diary. Then he went to sleep.

You know how I'm pretty much a ninja, right? Well, I used my super-sneaking skillz (with a Z, because I'm cool like that) to get into Sam's room and sneak a peek at his diary.

I KNOW, I KNOW! It wasn't the right thing to do, but I was just SO CURIOUS about whether he was going to go into the machine. Now that I've read it though, I feel really bad for him. Here's what he wrote.

Hi Diary,

Today Mum and Dad told me exactly what I've been wanting to hear for months! They finally said I could plug into the Happily Ever After machine FOREVER! It's just like I've been saying – it would be so much better if I didn't have to keep coming out into the real world.

In the Happily Ever After machine, I have friends, I feel special and important and I have a bunch of cool skills. I love being the best at something. And I like feeling like I'm helping people. I know I'm not actually helping because they're computer people, but I only know that once I'm unplugged from the machine.

The thing is, now that I've got the choice I wanted – to plug in forever – I'm not sure if I can do it. I'm not scared. I know I'd be happier in there, but I also know it would make Mum and Dad sad. I think they'd be heartbroken. They said they'd really miss me, but they want me to be happy.

Now I have to choose between making myself happy by hurting my parents' feelings, or staying here and being unhappy. It feels impossible to choose. Would it be selfish to make myself happy by hurting their feelings? Is it up to me to make my parents happy?

I don't know what to do...
Sam

Oh dear. Sorry if this report is a bit wet when it comes to you – I think I'm gonna cry! It all just seems so unfair!

Agent Mae signing out

SAM SHOULDN'T BE MISERABLE IF HE HAS THE CHANCE TO BE HAPPY, SHOULD HE? BUT IF HE DOES WHAT MAKES HIM HAPPY, HE'LL BREAK HIS PARENTS' HEARTS! WHAT SHOULD SAM DO?

INCOMING PHILOSO-MAIL

NEW MESSAGE

TO: AGENT MAE @ BRAINS TRUST
FROM: DR MATT @ SHORT & CURLY HQ
SUBJECT: DR MATT PHILOSO-MAIL

Mae! We've talked about using your sneaking skills responsibly! You can't go around snooping into people's diaries. It's like Spider-Man said: 'With great power comes great responsibility.'

I'm not sure it would be a good thing to use a stolen diary for research. Luckily for us though, it looks like after you left, Sam posted a copy of his diary entry onto his blog – *whambamthankyousam.com*. So seeing as Sam made his thoughts public, I guess it's OK for us to discuss them.

Let's start off with something we can all agree on: it's not always OK to chase your own happiness. Let's say you get your happiness from putting little spiky tacks on people's seats so they get a jab in the bum when they sit down. It would be wrong of you to do that, even if it made you happy. (It would probably be pretty funny too, but don't go messing with my chair at HQ!)

A philosopher named **Carol Gilligan** writes a lot about relationships and why they're important for ethics. She says we live in a world that's like a giant trampoline. When you move on the trampoline, it affects everybody. If you bounce really high, other people will get bounced too.

Life is similar. Our choices don't just affect us. They affect other people as well. In Sam's case, his decision to plug into Happily Ever After is going to be extremely painful for his mum and dad. Gilligan would probably tell Sam that he needs to think about his parents' feelings as well. Now would be the ideal time for Sam to use his **binoculars** and do some **fact finding** to learn what his parents think, how they could be affected and what they might want out of this situation.

Not every philosopher agrees with Carol though. Some think the only thing that matters is Sam's intention. He doesn't intend for his parents to be sad; he just wants to do something that will make him happy. As a side-effect of him being happy, his parents will be sad, but lots of people would say that's not his fault because he didn't choose to make his parents sad and he didn't *want* to make them sad. Unfortunately, there was no way for him to avoid making them sad while also making himself happy.

This idea is called **double-effect theory**. It's a bit fancy and complicated, but the idea is basically that when we do something, we cause lots of different things to happen. Some of them we want, some of them we don't. It would be impossible to do anything if we had to avoid any bad effects of what we do, so double-effect says sometimes it's OK to cause bad effects so long as we don't *want* them.

Here's another way to understand it – you've got a poisonous spider on your head (this is my worst nightmare; I'm getting scared just thinking it). Your friend might hit you on the head to squash the spider. It would probably hurt you, but that doesn't mean your friend did the wrong thing. So long as they weren't trying to hurt you and there was no better way of removing the spider, we'd say they did the right thing even though they hurt you.

Now, let's bring this back to Sam's situation.

Whether Sam should choose his happiness or his parents' happiness probably depends on his answers to a few questions.

1. We would need to know he doesn't want to hurt his parents' feelings. That's pretty obvious from the diary entry you so naughtily snuck from his room. So he gets a big tick here.

2. Does Sam's happiness outweigh his parents' sadness? This is pretty hard to know for sure, because it's difficult to measure something like happiness or sorrow. Given Sam's parents really love him, it might be tricky to argue that Sam's decision is going to do more good than harm, but it's possible. After all, Sam is going to live a life of *perfect* happiness in Happily Ever After, so maybe it's OK.

3. This is the trickiest one, are there any other ways for him to achieve happiness that don't end up hurting their feelings? Is Sam certain he couldn't be happy in the real world? The truth is, he probably can.

He might not be *as* happy as he would be in Happily Ever After, but there are probably changes he could make in his real life to improve things. He might change schools to somewhere he has more friends. He might start taking music lessons to chase his dream of becoming a rock star or he might join a volunteer group so he feels like he's helping out.

Happily Ever After is an example of what some people call **escapism** – when we use technology or entertainment to distract ourselves from the challenges of the real world. There's nothing wrong with being distracted or escaping every now and again. The poet **T. S. Eliot** understood this. He wrote that 'humankind cannot bear very much reality.'

As we get better and better at designing ways to escape – like virtual reality, reading novels or creating imaginary friends – we need to be careful. We shouldn't use escapism as a way of avoiding our lives and the hard work that's involved in achieving happiness. Ideally, nobody would need to plug into a machine in order to be happy.

Dr Matt signing out

THINKING QUESTIONS

1. Have you ever done something that hurt someone's feelings even though you weren't trying to?

2. Is it OK to be selfish sometimes? Do we always have to think about how our actions will affect other people?

3. What do you do to escape from real life? (Remember, it's OK to escape sometimes – we all do it!)

AUTHENTICITY: THE BEST LIFE OR THE REALEST LIFE?

A philosopher named **Robert Nozick** first wrote about The Experience Machine as a way of showing that most people do care about more than just pleasure. He proposed a machine exactly like Happily Ever After, where people could plug in for the rest of their lives and experience extreme happiness.

Nozick thought most people *wouldn't* plug in, he came to this conclusion because happiness isn't the only thing important to humans. We also care about **authenticity** – experiencing things as they really are. Most people tend to think authentic experiences are better than inauthentic (fake) experiences.

Here are a few questions to help you work out how much authenticity means to you:

1. Imagine your best friend isn't in fact your friend, they're just paid to be nice to you. Is it better to *actually* have a best friend, or is it just as good to have the *experience* of having a best friend, even if they're faking it?

2. Imagine you've been saving up for years to buy a really rare comic book. You finally have enough money to buy it, but when it arrives in the mail, it's a fake. You don't *know* it's a fake though. Is *thinking* you own a rare comic book as good as it would be if you *actually* owned the rare comic book?

3. Put yourself in Sam's shoes. You're a superstar musician and everybody in the crowd loves you. Except they're not a real crowd, they're just computer-generated people. Would it be better if Sam had *real* people cheering for him in the crowd?

AGENT DEBRIEF

NEW MESSAGE
TO: DR MATT @ SHORT & CURLY HQ
FROM: AGENT MAE @ BRAINS TRUST
SUBJECT: AGENT MAE – DEBRIEF FOR HQ

I feel so sorry for Sam and his parents. They're all being forced to choose between their happiness and somebody else's. If Sam prioritises his parents' feelings, he'll be left feeling sad in the real world. And his parents have already accepted a life with a lot of sorrow by offering Sam the chance to go into the machine. It sounds like, whatever happens, sadness is going to be inescapable. Which is ironic, seeing as that's exactly what the machine was designed to prevent!

But maybe that's the point: even if we spend our whole life trying to avoid being sad, we can't? Maybe part of what makes happiness so special is that it can be taken away so quickly? That's a depressing thought, but it's also kind of nice.

Still, whatever Sam chooses, it's going to bum me out, so I'm not going to stick around to see what happens. Before I come back to HQ, you have to promise you won't make me sit through another ethics class on respecting people's privacy. They go for SO long. Maybe I should just hop into Happily Ever After instead. Then I could be a REAL ninja.

Except not real . . . This stuff is weird!

Agent Mae signing out

LEARNING

SCHOOL'S OUT, FOREVER!

LUCY NGUYEN

FIELD RESEARCH REPORT:

SUBJECT: Lucy Nguyen

DETAILS: Student protester and curious cat.

NOTES:

- What's so good about learning?
- Do we need to go to school?

AGENT RABIA

REPORT RUN-DOWN

NEW MESSAGE

TO: DR MATT @ SHORT & CURLY HQ
FROM: AGENT RABIA @ BRAINS TRUST
SUBJECT: REPORT RUN-DOWN ON LUCY NGUYEN

I've heard stories about a student who has set up a protest at her school. She's sitting on the roof of the assembly hall and has a big sign saying, 'We don't need no education!' Her name is Lucy Nguyen. Apparently, last night she watched a movie called *Ferris Bueller's Day Off* and her dad showed her some of his old vinyl records, including one by a band called Pink Floyd. She says the movie and the song have made her decide school is really bad for students.

I've done some research into Pink Floyd. They had a famous song called 'Another Brick in the Wall (Part 2)' – weird name for a song if you ask me. It's all about how school controls our thinking and makes teachers seem totally mean. The video clip is super creepy. There are nasty teachers, kids are put into a factory and come out as faceless puppets. The video makes the education system look like a way of making everyone boring and the same. At the end, the kids rise up and destroy the school! (That part I liked.)

Lucy is saying similar things. I climbed up on the roof to talk to her about her protest. (I'm scared of heights, so this was extremely brave and I would like extra pudding at the next Brains Trust party, thanks.)

'I think I should be free to think for myself. School is just telling us what to think. Whenever we say something the teachers don't like, we get in

SIDE NOTE:

Is mind control real? I want to learn how to do it. For, you know, research. Definitely not to make my little brother give me his dessert. I know there's a fungus that attacks ants and can take control of their minds – is school fungus? So many questions – back to Lucy...

trouble and by the end of it, everyone thinks the same way. It's basically mind control,' she said. 'I think we should be able to learn about whatever we're interested in, get out of the classroom and have adventures. We don't need a desk, a laptop and a whiteboard to learn, we can learn anywhere!'

YEAH! GO, LUCY! I DO ALL MY LEARNING IN THE PARK AND AT THE MOVIES! I TOTALLY GET WHERE LUCY IS COMING FROM, BUT EVERYBODY SAYS SCHOOL IS IMPORTANT. I KNOW IT'S BORING, BUT IS SCHOOL REALLY BAD FOR US?

Agent Rabia signing out

WE DON'T NEED NO EDUCATION

INCOMING PHILOSO-MAIL

NEW MESSAGE

TO: AGENT RABIA @ BRAINS TRUST
FROM: DR MATT @ SHORT & CURLY HQ
SUBJECT: DR MATT PHILOSO-MAIL

You and Lucy sound like soulmates – using movies to form your ideas about ethics! Are you both members of some kind of secret movie club? Can I join?

Lucy sounds like a pretty committed thinker. I'm impressed – not only is she standing up for what she believes, she's also climbed what sounds like a scarily high building. What a daredevil! Plus, I think she might be on to something.

For a long time, philosophers have used their **brain-machetes** to **make a distinction** between **wisdom** and **knowledge**. Knowledge is usually specific – we know *about* something, like how old Tutankhamun was when he died or how many Pharaohs are buried in the Valley of the Kings in Egypt (19 years old and 63, thank you very much). But wisdom isn't just facts, it's much broader. Wisdom is basically 'knowing how to live well'. Someone who is wise might not know much trivia, but they'll know the kinds of things you need to live a good life.

Today, we don't think much about wisdom. We're interested in knowledge. We like people who are experts in a particular area (like ancient Egypt, or computer science, cooking or taking care of sick people), and we try to teach people so they can become experts in something. One of the reasons we do this is because it makes it easier for people to get jobs. How often do you get asked 'what do you want to do when you grow up?' This is sort of the way the school system works. It tries to give you the knowledge you'll need to get a job when you finish school.

That's not necessarily all bad. After all, in this society we need jobs to get money and we need money to survive! Plus, many people find a lot of meaning and happiness in their jobs. However, let's imagine if education wasn't just about jobs. What if we asked people 'what kind of person do you want to be when you grow up?' instead of 'what job do you want to do?' We'd give very different answers, wouldn't we? I know I'd probably list a bunch of different **virtues**. I'd want to be kind, patient, courageous, curious, artistic, know how to tell good stories, be able to get along with everyone and stuff like that. But that's not what school is designed to teach us: these days, we tend to learn these virtues from our friends, parents and community.

But if you were interested in those kinds of things or, like Lucy, you wanted to follow your own passions instead of what was on the curriculum, you might feel like you were being told who you should be when you grow up instead of being allowed to figure that out for yourself.

Dr Matt signing out

THINKING QUESTIONS

1. Should school help you to be a better person?

2. Can you **make a distinction** between 'getting an education' and 'going to school'?

3. Do you think school needs to be improved? If you think it does, what changes would you make?

FERRIS BUELLER'S DAY OFF

Ferris Bueller's Day Off is one of my all-time fave movies. It's about a teenager who skips school with his girlfriend, Sloane, and his best friend, Cameron. They have all kinds of adventures trying not to get caught by their principal, Ed Rooney.

Ferris, Sloane and Cameron sneak into a fancy restaurant for lunch, 'borrow' Cameron's dad's sports car and sing in a parade. Every now and again, you see their classmates falling asleep in class because it's so boring!

I wonder who learned more that day, the students who skipped school or the ones who stayed in class . . . ?

* P.S. If you want to watch *Ferris Bueller's Day Off* for yourself, make sure to check it's OK with your parents. It's rated PG.

RESEARCH UPDATE

NEW MESSAGE

TO: DR MATT @ SHORT & CURLY HQ

FROM: AGENT RABIA @ BRAINS TRUST

SUBJECT: RESEARCH UPDATE ON LUCY NGUYEN

Things have got interesting (and dangerous) now. Lots of other students have joined Lucy's protest. At first, the students who joined her in climbing up on the roof agreed with her. They wanted to be allowed to learn whatever they thought was interesting, instead of just being told what they should learn.

Just a second ago though, a bunch of other students climbed up and started demanding that the school be closed down. They're saying they don't want to learn anything at all. Lucy and her mates are now starting to get angry and it looks like a high-flying fight might break out between the two groups of protestors! Lucy's group are calling themselves the 'Curious Cats' and the other group (who don't really have a leader from the look of things) are calling themselves the 'Relaxed Red Pandas'.

This could be the cutest fight ever — like that movie *Cats and Dogs* but with red pandas. Actually, it could be pretty dangerous, seeing as they're not cats and red pandas, they're people. So maybe not so cute.

IS THERE A WAY FOR THEM TO FIGURE IT OUT? DO THE RED PANDAS HAVE A POINT? IS IT OK NOT TO WANT TO LEARN ANYTHING?

Agent Rabia signing out

INCOMING PHILOSO-MAIL

NEW MESSAGE

TO: AGENT RABIA @ BRAINS TRUST
FROM: DR MATT @ SHORT & CURLY HQ
SUBJECT: DR MATT PHILOSO-MAIL

At school I definitely had some friends who would have joined the Relaxed Red Pandas. They HATED school! They would chuck a sickie whenever they could, listen to music in class and sometimes even fall asleep. They definitely didn't think there was anything useful about learning.

Still, I wonder if the Relaxed Red Pandas and Curious Cats have more in common than they think. For example, lots of my friends didn't like coming to school, but they did like learning how to write code for websites, painting, getting better at the sports they enjoyed, reading books and inventing wacky gadgets and stuff like that.

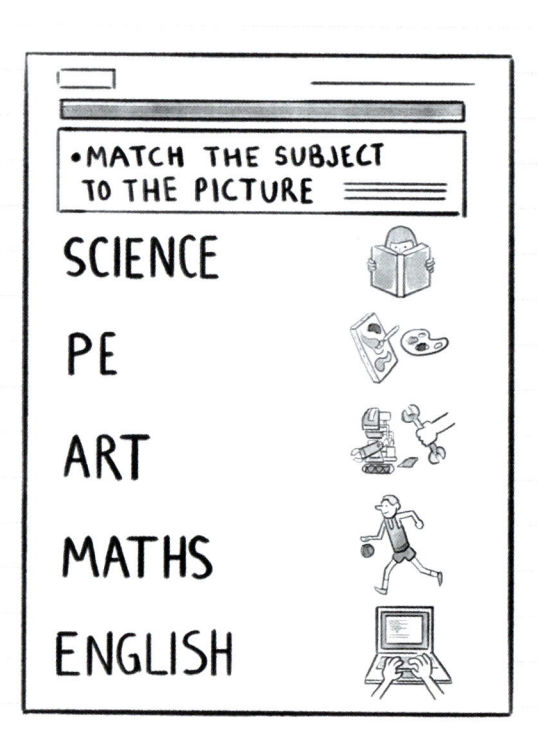

When you think about it, they were doing the kinds of things you learn at school. Coding is basically maths, painting is art, sport is PE, you read books in English and making inventions is basically science! So it wasn't the subjects they didn't like, it was the way they were forced to learn those subjects.

Some people like learning in a structured environment (which is what we usually mean when we say people are 'getting an education'), but some people don't. They like learning, but they don't like being forced into an 'education'. There's nothing wrong with that. People learn in all kinds of different ways, and that's part of what makes a teacher's job so challenging. Those who don't like structured learning aren't bad people – they're curious and want to know how the world works, just like the Curious Cats.

There might be people who don't want to learn anything at all. Some people might be happy so long as they're doing things that make themselves feel good. One reason to close down the school could be so everyone can play more video games or spend time hanging out next to the pool. So if what you care most about is feeling good and being happy, that kind of makes sense, doesn't it? After all, everyone loves video games and lazy days next to the pool!

Although I do wonder if, after a while, you'd get bored. One of the things that makes human beings what we are is our curiosity. We naturally want to discover new things, learn how stuff works and make sense of the world around us. Just like when we get a bit twitchy if we're cooped up all day and don't get out for some fresh air, we get bored and frustrated if we don't get chances to give our curiosity a workout.

If that's true, then I don't think it's a question of whether it's OK not to want to learn anything. I don't think it's even possible for a person not to want to learn anything, because curiosity is part of who we are.

A philosopher named **John Stuart Mill** once said, 'It is better to be Socrates dissatisfied than a pig satisfied'. What he meant was that humans have the ability to learn, think, create amazing art and tell knock-knock jokes (OK, maybe not that last one). He thought people were better off for having the ability to think and learn, even if it didn't make them happy.

Dr Matt signing out

THE PANOPTICON

Some people worry school is even more controlling than telling us we have to get a job when we grow up.

A British philosopher named **Jeremy Bentham** came up with a pretty mind-blowing invention that was all about control. It was called (fancy word alert) **The Panopticon**.

The word 'panopticon' basically means 'all seeing'. The Panopticon was Bentham's idea for a prison, where every prisoner can be seen from one central tower, but none of them could see the guard in the tower. Even though the prisoners wouldn't know if the guard was looking at them, the chance the guard *might* be looking at them would be enough to make them behave.

Why did he think this? Well, because the fear of being watched and seen doing the wrong thing is a good way to control people. It makes them act in a way that will keep them out of trouble. Pretty creepy, right?

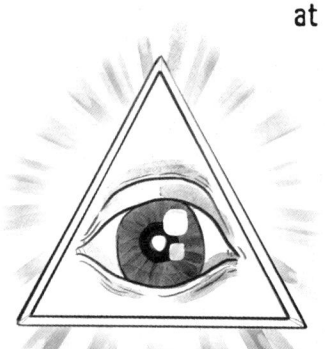

Many, many years later, the French philosopher **Michel Foucault** was worried that people might start designing schools like Bentham's Panopticon so they could keep watch on the students and keep them under control. Foucault thought this was a bad idea because it would make people act more 'normal' (which basically means 'boring').

So, like Lucy says, in theory you *could* make a school that was all about mind control if you wanted to. You'd just set the desks up so the students could all be seen by the teacher, but they wouldn't know when the teacher might decide to look at them.

I wonder if that sounds like your classroom. Hmmm . . .

THINKING QUESTIONS

1. Imagine the happiest pig in the world. Would you rather live your life as happy as that pig, but with no chance to learn or understand the world, or would you rather be a person, even if it means being bored, confused and maybe even having to go to school?

2. How do you like to learn? Do you like doing exams and assignments, or do you think you're at your best when you can go at your own pace?

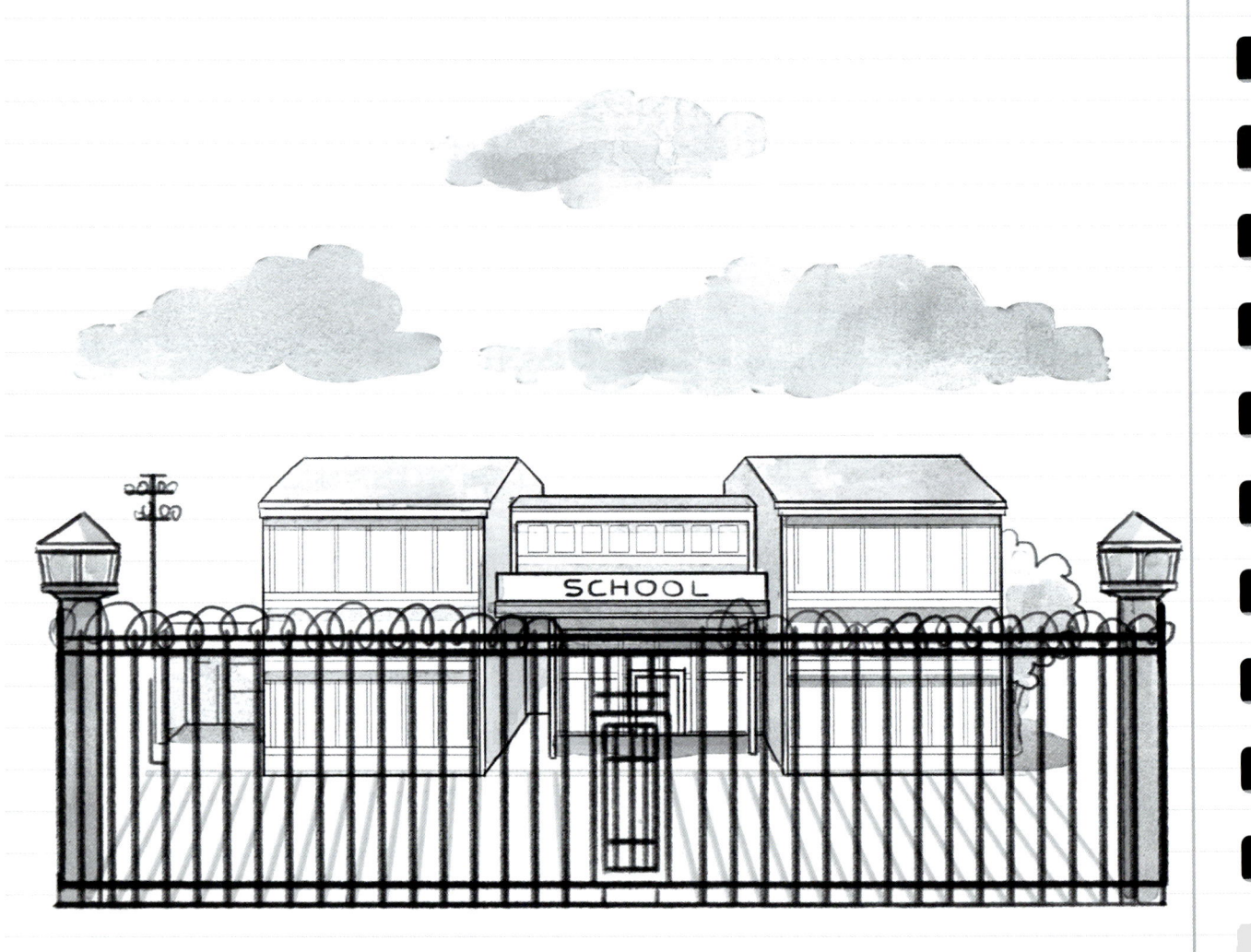

AGENT DEBRIEF

NEW MESSAGE

TO: DR MATT @ SHORT & CURLY HQ
FROM: AGENT RABIA @ BRAINS TRUST
SUBJECT: AGENT RABIA – DEBRIEF FOR HQ

If I were at Lucy's school, I think I'd be part of the Curious Cats. I love finding out new things about the world and seeing how it all works, but stuff like learning spelling and doing creative writing isn't for me. I wish I could just do science all the time!

Even people who have finished school have to ask themselves whether they want to learn things that are going to help them get a better job, or if they want to spend their time doing things that make them wise or fulfil their curiosity.

With all this in mind, I'm finding it hard to see where the Relaxed Red Pandas are coming from, but if I use my **torch** to imagine what they might be thinking and feeling, I can sort of understand. If I felt about every subject the way I feel about spelling and creative writing, I probably wouldn't want to go to school either. I wonder if the Relaxed Red Pandas really hate learning, or if they just haven't found something they're interested in yet.

Anyway, I hope they get down from that roof soon – I hate heights! Watching them all up there was giving me the heebie-jeebies! I think I'll need a bowl of popcorn and a DVD of *Ferris Bueller's Day Off* to calm my nerves when I get back to HQ. Can you fire up the microwave for me?

Agent Rabia signing out

LIFE CHOICES
yes
No
Probably not
Perhaps
Maybe
Nuh!
Of course!

THE VAMPIRE BOOTH

JACK YOOLA

FIELD RESEARCH REPORT:

SUBJECT: Jack Yoola

DETAILS: Able to turn other people into vampires.

NOTES:

- How should we make decisions we can't take back?
- Would it be good to live forever?

AGENT ARJUN

REPORT RUN-DOWN

NEW MESSAGE
TO: DR MATT @ SHORT & CURLY HQ
FROM: AGENT ARJUN @ BRAINS TRUST
SUBJECT: REPORT RUN-DOWN ON JACK YOOLA

The circus has come to town and I just love the circus! Thanks for sending me on this assignment. It's got all the typical circus things I adore — fried food, colourful outfits, the awesome hall of mirrors and the Ferris wheel (which always smells a little bit like vomit). But this circus has something I've never seen before. Something weird. Something SPOOOOOOKY.

I was just exploring the circus looking for a deep-fried Mars bar (you've got to try one), when I came across this weird booth where you pay a dollar and get bitten on the neck! I've heard of 'kissing booths' before (which sound pretty unhygienic if you ask me), but this is different. Instead of an awkward kiss, you get nibbled on the neck.

Oh, also, the bite on the neck turns you into a vampire. I should probably have mentioned that bit earlier, shouldn't I? VAMPIRES ARE REAL . . . who knew?!

The guy who runs the booth is named Jack Yoola (that name sounds familiar for some reason). He's got loads of signs up saying why being a vampire is so awesome, and he's really keen to tell everyone at the circus. 'More energy! Wear super-cool clothes! Party all night long! Have super-senses! Jump higher, run faster, turn into a bat! And best of all, you get to live forever!'

There are also a bunch of TVs at the booth playing interviews with people who have become vampires. They all seem to love it.

'I never imagined becoming a vampire would make me so happy. It's the best decision I ever made.'

'Now that I'm a vampire, I understand how lame it is to be a human. Imagine not being able to see during the night. Boooring!'

'It's impossible to explain what being a vampire is like. You just have to try it!'

There's one catch: once you're a vampire, there's no turning back. Also, you have to drink a bit of blood, but they put it into a smoothie and it's apparently delicious.

It all sounds pretty great. I know you sent me here to observe what's happening, but I've made my choice – I'm gonna sign up. Oh man! I spent my last dollar on a marshmallow shaped like a pig. I named him Ham. He was so cute, but then I ate him . . . Sorry, Ham!

WITHOUT A DOLLAR, I GUESS I CAN'T BE A VAMPIRE, BUT MAYBE THAT'S A GOOD THING? I MEAN, BEING A VAMPIRE SOUNDS COOL, BUT IT'S A TOTALLY DIFFERENT WAY OF LIVING – WHAT IF IT TURNED OUT I DIDN'T LIKE IT? I'D BE STUCK LIKE THAT FOREVER!

==Agent Arjun signing out==

INCOMING PHILOSO-MAIL

NEW MESSAGE

TO: AGENT ARJUN @ BRAINS TRUST
FROM: DR MATT @ SHORT & CURLY HQ
SUBJECT: DR MATT PHILOSO-MAIL

Blood smoothies, huh? That's creepy and gross. Being a vampire sounds great!

Delicious smoothies aside, you're asking the right questions about becoming a vampire. Usually, when we're trying to decide how to live our lives, there's one basic question we ask ourselves: will it make me happy?

Let's pretend you're trying to decide whether to play netball or tennis next season. Whichever way you make the decision, what you're really trying to figure out is which sport is more likely to make you happy.

Well, here are a few tricks to help you choose:

1. Find some people who play netball and tennis and ask them if it makes them happy. Even better, if a few of your friends play netball or tennis, you could ask them. Because they're your friends, there's a better chance they'll have similar interests to you.

2. Try playing both netball and tennis for a little while and then decide which one you liked better.

3. Imagine what your life would be like if you played either netball or tennis. For example, you could imagine what it would be like playing a team sport versus an individual sport and decide which one you liked better.

The reason these strategies work is because, even if we've never played tennis or netball before, we've probably experienced enough things *similar*

to tennis and netball to imagine what it's like.

Unfortunately, that's not the case with becoming a vampire – this isn't like anything else you've ever experienced. It's completely new. It's something that transforms us in ways we can't imagine or understand until after we've been transformed. That's why one of the vampires said, 'It's impossible to say what it's like'.

Even if being a vampire made our friends happy, we can't know if we'd feel the same way. We can't 'practise' being a vampire before we sign up, so it would be impossible to *imagine* what being a vampire is like with any accuracy.

If all our usual tricks are useless, how should we make up our minds?

We need to find something to base our decision on other than happiness. We can't know if becoming a vampire will make us happy, so we need to think about it in some other way. There are a couple of options.

First, we could make the decision based on what we *know* about becoming a vampire. We know it gives you super-speed and the ability to stay up all night, so if you knew super-speed would be useful to you – say, you wanted to become a superhero or an awesome pizza delivery person – then you might be able to use that to make the decision. However, you'd have to know that, even though you'd be getting superpowers, there might be downsides you hadn't thought of, and you'd have to be OK with that.

Second, we could make the decision based on **curiosity**. Imagine life as though you were an explorer off on an adventure: you don't know what you'll find or discover about the world and yourself, but that's part of the fun!

When it comes to curiosity, the only question is, do you want to find out what being a vampire is like? It's OK if you don't – nobody says we *have* to discover everything there is to discover.

Dr Matt signing out

THINKING QUESTIONS

1. Is there something you'd love to try, but you're too scared to because you're not sure what it would be like?

2. Have you ever done something you couldn't take back?

3. What would life be like if we didn't try new things, take risks or make discoveries?

ARE ALL VAMPIRES BAD?

If you're a vampire and you've got something stuck in your teeth, you might never know! That's because, according to legends, vampires have no reflection.

This idea comes from *Dracula* – the book published by Bram Stoker in 1897, where the most famous vampire in history, Dracula, got his big break. In the story, vampires are said not to have a soul, which is why they don't have a reflection.

At the time Stoker was writing, not having a soul was seen as a pretty bad thing. Nowadays, we use the world 'soulless' to mean something is nasty and uncaring. So even before a vampire had *done* anything bad, they were already seen as bad just because of who they were.

Still, it makes you wonder: if they can't see their reflection, how come they always have such great hair?

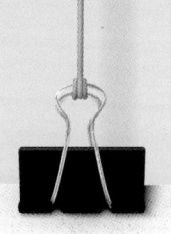

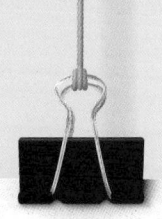

LAURIE PAUL

The first (and only) philosopher to think about becoming a vampire is a woman named Laurie Paul. She works at a university called UNC Chapel Hill, in the USA.

Laurie uses the vampire example as a **thought experiment** to get us to think about all kinds of life-changing experiences. And there's one thing your parents have definitely done, which she thinks is a lot like becoming a vampire: having kids!

Even though having kids doesn't sound anywhere near as exciting as becoming a super-cool creature of the night, Laurie thinks they're pretty similar. Just like it's impossible to imagine being a vampire, it's impossible to imagine being a parent.

Remember we said there are three ways you could test an experience to see if it would make you happy: ask other people, try it out first or imagine what it would be like. Laurie thinks none of these work for parenting.

We can't know for sure whether parenting will make us happy or not. Just because it makes other people happy (or sad) doesn't mean the same will be true for us. The kind of love parents have for their kids isn't one we can understand until we've experienced it.

Plus, you can't try out parenting and then change your mind – once you're a parent, you're a parent for life!

RESEARCH UPDATE

NEW MESSAGE

TO: DR MATT @ SHORT & CURLY HQ
FROM: AGENT ARJUN @ BRAINS TRUST
SUBJECT: RESEARCH UPDATE ON JACK YOOLA

I've managed to get an interview with Jack Yoola himself! I'm going to ask him some questions about what it's like to be a vampire.

Agent Arjun: Jack! Jack! Hey, over here! Hi – can I ask you some questions?

Jack: Sure, only if you give me your sandwich.

Agent Arjun: My sandwich? But I'm really hungry . . . I guess you could have half?

Jack: Nope. Give me all of it, or no interview.

Agent Arjun: OK, fine. That's a bit selfish though.

Jack: Listen, when you're a vampire and you can live forever, you don't worry about stuff like 'being good' or 'doing the right thing', you just do whatever you want.

Agent Arjun: My sandwich is awesome.

Jack: I wouldn't know. Vampires don't eat food. I'm just gonna chuck it in the rubbish.

Agent Arjun: Wait! I was going to eat that! Oh . . . it's in the bin.

Jack: Yep, it was MY sandwich and I can do whatever I want with it.

Agent Arjun: Don't you feel bad when you're selfish? Wouldn't it feel better to be nice?

Jack: Nah. Sometimes when I've done something bad I feel guilty for a while, but I live forever, so eventually I forget what I did and just keep on being awesome! Honestly though – the 'NO ETHICS' part of being a vampire is probably my favourite part.

Agent Arjun: OK. Thanks for your time, I guess.

Jack: Whatever, nerd.

INTERVIEW ENDS

WHAT. A. MEANIE!

I CAN'T BELIEVE HE TOOK MY SANDWICH AND THEN THREW IT IN THE BIN! IN THE BIN! IF BEING IMMORTAL MAKES YOU HORRIBLE, THEN I DEFINITELY DON'T WANT TO BE A VAMPIRE.

WHY WOULD BEING IMMORTAL MAKE YOU SUCH AN AWFUL PERSON?

Agent Arjun signing out

INCOMING PHILOSO-MAIL

NEW MESSAGE

TO: AGENT ARJUN @ BRAINS TRUST
FROM: DR MATT @ SHORT & CURLY HQ
SUBJECT: DR MATT PHILOSO-MAIL

Oh, Arjun, I'm so sorry. Your poor sandwich – a victim in our noble research quest. We will keep asking questions, we will keep researching. Your sandwich did not die in vain. (I'll also make you another one when you get back to HQ.)

Lots of people see immortality as a good thing because it allows us to spend more time doing the stuff we love. However, imagine if you'd been alive for so long that all the good things in life had become MEGA boring. What if you'd seen it all, done it all and learned it all? And now you were tired, bored and had stopped caring. If that was the case, would it be a good thing to live forever?

Think about it like this. I LOVE ice cream. If you gave me a bowl of ice cream, I'd gobble it up and want more. If you brought me a second bowl, I'd gobble that up too. Maybe I'd still want more (even though I was feeling a bit sick). After a while, if you kept giving me ice cream, I'd start to lose interest. I'd be so full of the stuff, even the idea of it would make me feel sick. I wouldn't want ice cream anymore. In fact, I wouldn't even *care* about it anymore.

A philosopher named **Bernard Williams** made a similar argument. He said if we lived long enough, we'd run out of things to live for. But not everyone agrees with him – let's go back to the ice cream example.

After chowing down on way too much ice cream, I might not want it for a while. But later (after a nap and some savoury chips), I'm probably going to start finding ice cream delicious again. Maybe the same is true about immortality: we might get bored of something for a while, but then it would get interesting again. As the years went on, there'd be new things to invent, jumpers to knit, little fluffy bunnies to cuddle . . . the list goes on.

However, Jack Yoola agrees with Bernard Williams. He seems to have stopped caring, which helps us understand why he's acting like such a meanie.

Ethics is about trying to live well and do the right thing, but most people agree that it's only possible because we care for people and things. If we didn't see any value in *anything*, we wouldn't be able to tell the difference between good and bad. With that in mind I wonder if it's possible to live for so long that you stop caring and stop thinking about good and bad.

Philosophers have spent *a lot* of time writing about death. (We're not much fun at parties.) Most of them agree that death is scary and unpleasant, but it's one of the things that gives meaning to our lives.

One of my favourite quotes comes from Benjamin Franklin, one of the founding fathers of the United States. He said (basically), 'If you don't want to be forgotten after you die, either write things worth reading or do things worth remembering.' If he's right, then death really matters. It's what makes us want to be helpful, creative, courageous and kind – so our lives will keep mattering even after we're gone.

If we could live forever, would we lose that motivation?

Dr Matt signing out

THINKING QUESTIONS

1. Can you think of a time when you had too much of a good thing? How did you feel about it after your binge session? Did it still make you happy?

2. Do you think you'd eventually turn into a horrible person if you lived forever?

FUN FACTS: THE IMMORTAL JELLYFISH

Did you know there is an immortal creature on earth right now?

Turritopsis nutricula, more commonly known as the **Immortal Jellyfish**, is tiny. At their biggest, they're only half a centimetre long, but what they lack in size they make up for in stamina. See, *Turritopsis nutricula* (her mates call her Turry) can technically live forever.

This is because Turry has two different life stages. First, the polypoid stage, when the jellyfish is just a baby – it's just a teeny stalk with tentacles that it uses to get food. After a while, it grows to the second stage, called the medusa stage. At this point, Turry is ready to have kids, minus the tentacles – sounds pretty normal, right?

It is. Except if Turry is having a tough time feeding itself in the more complex second stage, it can just reverse itself back into a little feeding tentacle. Basically, it turns back into a baby! How good would that be? Whenever you're tired or don't want to do your homework, BAM, you're a baby again.

It also means Turry can live forever.

VAMPIRE-THEMED ICE CREAM FLAVOURS

BLOOD ORANGE · CHOMPOLATE CHIP · TROPICAL FANGO · BITER-SCOTCH

Vein-illa · STRAWBERRY CHEESE-CAPE · Neck-opolitan · COOKIES & SCREAM

AGENT DEBRIEF

NEW MESSAGE

TO: DR MATT @ SHORT & CURLY HQ
FROM: AGENT ARJUN @ BRAINS TRUST
SUBJECT: AGENT ARJUN – DEBRIEF FOR HQ

Becoming a vampire still sounds pretty sweet in a lot of ways, but the trickiness of making life-changing decisions is scary. I've been thinking over all the big decisions I'm going to have to make in my life: will I be a parent when I grow up? Should I join the army? Move to another country? Accept a pro sports contract? These are massive decisions!

I've also been reading up on a few scientists who are actually trying to make people immortal (without turning them into vampires). Some of their ideas are very weird – like uploading everyone's brains into a computer so we become a kind of giant super-brain. Others are trying to reverse the ageing process in our bodies so we can keep partying for eternity. It's all whizz-bang science stuff, but now I'm not sure if it would make us happier.

All this thinking about big decisions has made me so HUNGRY – get started on my sandwich, I'll be back at HQ soon!

Agent Arjun signing out

LETTING GO

SAYING GOODBYE TO THE WHISKERS GANG

SAMAR KHAN

FIELD RESEARCH REPORT:

SUBJECT: Samar Khan

DETAILS: Has too much stuff to fit into her new bedroom, so has to make some sacrifices.

NOTES:

- Why do we get emotionally attached to objects?
- Should we always be loyal?
- Can you betray something that isn't alive?

AGENT KOA

REPORT RUN-DOWN

NEW MESSAGE
TO: DR MATT @ SHORT & CURLY HQ
FROM: AGENT KOA @ BRAINS TRUST
SUBJECT: REPORT RUN-DOWN ON SAMAR KHAN

Samar's family is moving house. Her mum's got a new job and they're going to move closer to the city to make it easier for her to get to work. Samar is really excited to move. She'll still be near her friends and the new house is closer to the beach. Plus, she'll have her own room for the first time!

There's only one catch. Samar's room is pretty small. There won't be much space for all her stuff. Samar has lots of books, a desk she uses to write her own stories and a huge collection of soft, adorable, fluffy seals. They're super cute – each one has different colours and outfits. She calls them 'The Whiskers Gang'. It's honestly the biggest collection I've ever seen. I think she could probably throw away her bed and just sleep on the toys – that's how many there are!

Samar has to decide what she's going to keep and what she'll chuck. It's an impossible decision. She uses her desk all the time for writing – she wants to be a writer when she finishes school – so she can't get rid of that. Her books are her inspiration, and lots of them belong to the family, so it's not her decision to throw them out (plus, they look cool on the shelf). Samar doesn't play with The Whiskers Gang much anymore, they just collect dust on her shelf. But all of them are special to her.

Most of them were presents from her friends and family. Samar bought a few for herself after important moments in her life – winning the netball grand final, before she had an operation when she broke her arm, after her grandpa passed away . . . stuff like that. She doesn't use them anymore, but they're still important to her in a different way to the desk or the books.

Her parents have suggested Samar could give The Whiskers Gang to the little boy and girl who live next door and who really love playing with the seals, but Samar's not sure. She tried to explain to her parents, 'It doesn't feel right to give them away. They're part of me!'

I don't think Samar's parents understand, but I do. When I go for walks on the beach with my aunty, we always pick up one stone – the smoothest, most interestingly coloured one we can find – and keep it in a collection. I don't look at it very often, but I wouldn't ever want to get rid of it. I just feel better knowing it's there. But all the same, my rocks – like Samar's seals – are useless. She has to choose between keeping things she still uses and keeping something she doesn't need. Plus, in giving them away she could make two other kids very happy.

IS IT SELFISH OR SILLY OF SAMAR TO HOLD ON TO THE WHISKERS GANG? HOW DO WE FIGURE OUT WHAT STUFF IS IMPORTANT AND WHAT STUFF ISN'T?

Agent Koa signing out

INCOMING PHILOSO-MAIL

NEW MESSAGE

TO: AGENT KOA @ BRAINS TRUST
FROM: DR MATT @ SHORT & CURLY HQ
SUBJECT: DR MATT PHILOSO-MAIL

Do you want to know a secret? I still have a teddy bear from when I was a baby!

Well, OK, he's not actually a teddy bear, he's a dinosaur. His name is Dino, and he's modelled on a character from a kids' cartoon called *The Flintstones*, where a Stone Age family have a pet dinosaur.

I used to take Dino everywhere. I needed to have him to fall asleep and wherever I moved, even as I finished high school and university, I kept Dino. A lot of the time he'd be kept in a safe place rather than living on my bed, but I could NEVER throw him away. Some things are important to us because of the way we feel about them – they have **sentimental value**. 'Sentiment' is a fancy word for feelings.

I completely understand what Samar is going through. Working out what to keep and give up isn't easy, and it's a difficult decision only we can make for ourselves. A lot of what makes something important is up to us.

One of the superpowers people have is our ability to care for things. When we care about something, we've decided it's important – sometimes without even being aware of it!

A philosopher named **John Locke** thought that when we own something, it's special because we've put a little bit of ourselves into it. Maybe we worked hard to build it, maybe we saved up our money to buy it or maybe we spent a lot of time and creativity inventing something new.

Locke didn't think we had to care about everything we owned, but his ideas are useful for understanding *why* some objects seem so special to us. It could be because we've spent so much time with them that we've filled them with our stories, our effort and our memories. This makes them hard to replace – just like we couldn't replace one of our arms, sometimes it's hard to imagine what it would be like to live without some of our stuff. We become attached to it, which means we don't feel safe or complete when it's not around.

One group of philosophers think attachment is a really bad idea. They're called **Stoics** – they started out in ancient Greece, but they're still around today. The Stoics think *all* attachment is bad because it always makes us suffer.

Whether we're attached to objects, people or anything we can't control, we set ourselves up for pain because those things we care about will eventually break, die or disappear from our lives. Basically, feelings, sentiments and attachments are a guaranteed path to suffering and sadness.

Stoicism has a lot of things in common with some other ideas systems, like **Buddhism**. Stoics think the only thing we should care about is whether we're a good person or not. We can always control what choice we make – whether to be kind or selfish, brave or cowardly, patient or impatient and so on (at least, that's what the Stoics say). So long as all we care about is the choices we make, we'll always be in control of our own happiness.

The Stoics would probably say Samar would be happier without *any* of her stuff. They'd also suggest Samar should be more concerned with doing something kind, like giving away the toys.

Remember, in ethics we use our **hiking poles** to **question our emotions**. We know Samar is attached to The Whiskers Gang. The question is: is attachment a good thing or a bad thing?

Dr Matt signing out

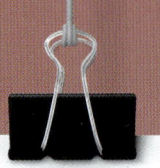

THE ORIGINAL TEDDY BEARS

There aren't many toys people love more than their first teddy. But do you know where teddy bears came from?

The story of the teddy bear actually starts with a man trying to be ethical. And not just any man – former US President **Theodore 'Teddy' Roosevelt!**

Yep, the teddy bear is named after a US President. Here's how it happened:

Teddy Roosevelt was a well-known hunter. He loved it and, according to historical records, he was pretty good at it too. But on one trip in 1902, he was having no luck at all. The President and a group of hunters had travelled to Mississippi and were looking for bears. Everyone except Roosevelt had successfully hunted one (how embarrassing).

A few members of his hunting party decided to help him out. They cornered a black bear and tied it to a tree. Then they offered Roosevelt the chance to shoot it so he wouldn't leave the hunt empty-handed. This might sound horrible to you, and hunting is pretty ethically controversial, but Roosevelt thought it was a really good way of getting close to nature. Believe it or not, lots of hunters are very fond of animals and the environment!

Roosevelt wouldn't do it. As a hunter, part of what he valued was the chase, and part of what made it fair, in his eyes, was that the animals always had a chance to fight back or escape. He didn't see anything fair about killing a defenceless bear.

This news spread to newspapers all over the country. It was a great story and a real insight into the personality of the President. Two people who read the story were a couple of toy makers called **Morris and Rose Michtom**. They specialised in making stuffed toys, and wrote to Roosevelt asking to make a toy bear in his honour. The President gave them his permission, so they started making 'Teddy's Bears'.

And the rest is history.

RESEARCH UPDATE

NEW MESSAGE

TO: DR MATT @ SHORT & CURLY HQ
FROM: AGENT KOA @ BRAINS TRUST
SUBJECT: RESEARCH UPDATE ON SAMAR KHAN

BREAKING NEWS! Samar decided to give The Whiskers Gang away. She took some lovely photos of the collection and held on to one special member of the gang to remember them all. She's said her goodbyes and passed them on so they can make some other kids happy. That's really kind of her. The kids next door were over the moon; I can still hear them playing with their new seals.

That's all well and good, but Samar's devastated. She's been lying on her bed having a good cry for over an hour. Her mum came in to check on her and see what the matter was. She gave Samar a big hug and told her how proud she was that her daughter had done something so kind, generous and thoughtful.

It didn't have much effect on Samar's mood. She's still down in the dumps, she won't eat anything and just wants to be alone. I'm wondering if the Stoics were right — if this is what happens when you love toys, maybe you're better off not loving at all.

This makes me think of the time I was working on a painting. I was using one of my favourite photos, which was taken on our family camping holiday in the bush. I used to look at it every day. We were all so happy — it's like a perfect memory for me. But while I was working on my painting, I accidentally spilled paint all over the photo. It was totally ruined and I was so upset. I knew I hadn't done anything wrong, but I was still inconsolable. The Stoics would say I shouldn't care, so long as I was being a good person. Thinking about it like that kind of makes sense to me.

IF SAMAR WAS TRYING TO DO SOMETHING GOOD, WHY DOES SHE STILL FEEL BAD ABOUT IT? HOW COME SOMETIMES WE GET UPSET EVEN WHEN WE HAVEN'T DONE ANYTHING WRONG?

Agent Koa signing out

INCOMING PHILOSO-MAIL

NEW MESSAGE

TO: AGENT KOA @ BRAINS TRUST
FROM: DR MATT @ SHORT & CURLY HQ
SUBJECT: DR MATT PHILOSO-MAIL

Koa, you're asking exactly the kind of questions a Stoic would want you to ask. And you're right, a Stoic would say Samar has no reason to feel upset because she did something good. She was kind and kindness is a **virtue** – a trait that reflects good character. Stoics are big on virtue because they think it's the only thing we can control.

Here's a brain-wrinkling thought for you: what if we *shouldn't* try to control everything? What if it's just an inescapable fact that lots of the things we care about aren't within our control? Then the whole idea of Stoicism would be based on a mistake!

A philosopher named **Martha Nussbaum** (secret confession: she's one of my favourite philosophers) argued that everything we care about can be taken away from us. That sounds horrible, but she thinks it's actually sort of beautiful. She says part of loving something is being vulnerable – loving it *so much* that if we lost it we would be completely heartbroken. And that kind of makes sense, in a way.

If part of what it means to be human is to feel and to care, then the goal of Stoicism seems to be to make us less like humans and more like robots. Here's a question for you – is it important to care about stuff so much that we can be heartbroken if something bad happens to it?

Let's unpack this with a **thought experiment** – **maps** at the ready!

Imagine it's Saturday arvo and it's the footy Grand Final! There are two kids at the big game, they are both really excited because their team has made the final and they are both HUGE fans! After a super close, intense match, their team loses. One of the kids starts to cry, is bummed out for a week, eventually gets over it, but still gets upset if it comes up in conversation. The other kid shrugs, says, 'Well, I knew there was a chance they might lose', and gets on with their day.

Which kid would you say is a better fan? Who loves the team more? If you thought it was the first kid, it might be because you think our emotions and vulnerability are an important part of what makes us human. Maybe you think there are some things we *should* feel, even if they are uncomfortable or make us suffer. Or maybe you think the second kid sounds more sensible because they didn't blow a footy game totally out of proportion. In which case maybe you're a little bit of a Stoic.

In Samar's case, it seems like it might be a good thing she's so upset. It shows she appreciated and got the most out of her toys. She loved them so much it's broken her heart to see them go. That's not a sign she did the wrong thing, it's just that if you care about something, it hurts to say goodbye.

When we haven't done anything wrong but we still feel bad about our actions, we have what philosopher **Rosalind Hursthouse** calls a **moral remainder** ('moral' is basically another word for 'ethical'). A moral remainder is a bit like when you do divisions in maths. When something doesn't divide perfectly into something else, you have a few extra numbers left over – that's the remainder.

Sometimes an ethical puzzle is too complex to solve perfectly. There's stuff (or emotions) left over that leaves us feeling like we did the wrong thing, even if we didn't. Samar isn't feeling bad because it was wrong to give away her toys – she's feeling bad because, even though she did the right thing, doing what's right isn't always easy.

Dr Matt signing out

THINKING QUESTIONS

1. Is there something in your life you absolutely couldn't give away? Why is it important to you?

2. The more we care about things, the more upset we get when we lose them. Would it be better not to care about stuff at all?

3. If you were Samar, what would you have given away to make more space in your bedroom? The Whiskers Gang, the books or the writing desk? Why?

4. There's an old saying: 'It's better to have loved and lost than never to have loved at all'. Do you agree, or is it sometimes better to avoid pain, even if it means we try not to care so much about stuff?

HOW TO BE A STOIC

Stoicism is a very old idea, but lots of people still try to live like them today. They value living their lives without being so caught up in things they can't control: what other people think about them, whether they have as much stuff as they'd like or whether there's enough chicken salt on their hot chips (OK, that might just be me).

If you'd like to be more of a Stoic, here are some ways to get started:*

1. **Prepare for the worst:** Stoics think an effective way to avoid being totally caught up in your emotions when something bad happens is by imagining the worst thing that could happen in advance. That way, you're not surprised if it actually happens! Let's say you've got a big test coming up. A Stoic would take some time out in the morning to imagine walking into the exam room and not being able to remember a single thing. Then, if you do forget a few answers, you'll already be mentally and emotionally prepared.

2. **Plan to be good:** Think about the challenges you're going to face during the day. Try to work out how to do the right thing in those situations and imagine what the best version of yourself would do in those moments.

3. **Know what you can change:** To be a good Stoic, you have to understand what you can control and what you can't. You can waste a lot of time and energy if you place importance on things you can't control. Before you do something, ask: is it possible for me to change what's going to happen? If it's not, find something else to do.

4. **See the big picture:** Stoics believe they are a very small part in a very big universe. They think we should be concerned about other people in our family, community and the entire world! However, we shouldn't let our concern turn into suffering: remember, only worry about what you can change.

5. **Reflect on your day:** At the end of the day, think back over what you did. How often did you do something good? Did you have any stuff-ups? Think about what happened and why you did the wrong thing, and make some notes to change them tomorrow. Then sleep it off and do it all again!

*Some of these tips came from philosopher **Massimo Pigliucci's** super-handy website 'How to be a Stoic'. Thanks, Massimo!

AGENT DEBRIEF

NEW MESSAGE
TO: DR MATT @ SHORT & CURLY HQ
FROM: AGENT KOA @ BRAINS TRUST
SUBJECT: AGENT KOA – DEBRIEF FOR HQ

Sometimes life just seems unfair, doesn't it? Samar did a really kind thing and still got left feeling rotten about it! There's no reward – but I guess she didn't do it for the reward.

Maybe Samar's feelings are just part of her saying goodbye. They're not good or bad, they're just feelings. I wonder if Stoics get so focused on feelings being bad and causing suffering that they forget that feelings like sadness aren't always bad. In a weird way, they're actually kind of nice, like when you remember something you love that's gone now.

Still, I can see how the Stoics help us to be careful and not get too caught up with our feelings. It might be good to let ourselves get down in the dumps or excited sometimes, but after a while, we need to let it go.

Hmm . . . 'Let it Go' is a great name for a song. Has anyone written anything like that? Probably not. OK, I'm gonna start writing some music – see you later!

Agent Koa signing out

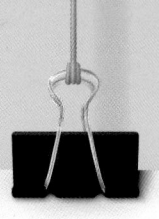

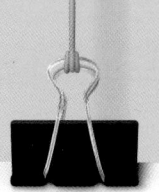

FAIRNESS

THE HIGHS AND LOWS OF BEING TALL

JUAN RODRIGUEZ

FIELD RESEARCH REPORT:

SUBJECT: Juan Rodriguez

DETAILS: Tallest boy in the world (3 m tall – slightly shorter than an Asian elephant).

NOTES:

- Is he being treated fairly?
- Should lots of people be interrupted to make life easier for one person?
- How do we define what's normal?

AGENT MAE

REPORT RUN-DOWN

NEW MESSAGE
TO: DR MATT @ SHORT & CURLY HQ
FROM: AGENT MAE @ BRAINS TRUST
SUBJECT: REPORT RUN-DOWN ON JUAN RODRIGUEZ

Our highly sophisticated social media monitoring identified a potential new research subject . . . OK, fine, I was online instead of working. Anyway, it's lucky I was, because I came across this boy who is a real-life giant! His name is Juan Rodriguez and he's three metres tall. His story has gone viral because he just started a YouTube vlog (maybe he should call it 'Juan's tall tales' – get it? Tall tales? Because he's tall? Hilarious!).

He's posted videos about how he eats breakfast. He uses a bucket as a cereal bowl and eats with a little gardening shovel. How awesome is that? I'm definitely asking my mum if I can start doing that from now on. But some of the things he posts about aren't so fun. His family have had to spend a lot of money on specially-designed transport and furniture because he can't fit into standard-sized cars or catch the bus to school, and he can't sit comfortably in ordinary chairs or fit his legs under tables. In a recent video, he said:

'People think I must have a great life. I'm in the Guinness World Records, always get good views at concerts and all the rest, but it's not all fun. I'd love to ride the bus with my friends, be able to go watch a movie and sit in the same cinema seats as everybody else and be able to eat in at my fave Chinese restaurant instead of always having to get takeaway. But people don't think about what I need to get through the day. Society wasn't built with people like me in mind, and a lot of the time it feels really unfair.'

After watching that, I felt so sad for Juan. I had to watch a bunch of clips of penguins chasing each other just to feel better. Then I decided to go see what life is like for Juan firsthand. I found him at school, sitting in what looked like an especially boring history class with a teacher who looked like an ogre (or maybe he was an ogre who looked like a teacher? Who knows . . .).

Juan was sitting in the middle of the class. His knees were so high they were lifting his desk off the floor. At one point, he raised his hand to ask a question and stuck his hand straight into the ceiling fan. O-U-C-H! The whole class started laughing and the cranky ogre sent Juan to the principal's office for 'being a distraction'. Talk about unfair. He didn't do anything wrong.

The principal told Juan he understood things were difficult, but that there was nothing she could do for him. If she bought him a bigger desk, she'd be giving him 'special treatment', which wouldn't be fair to the other students. She made a pretty good point: even though Juan is the tallest person in the class by a lot, there are other tall students who find the desks uncomfortable. She also said the cost of making the school more comfortable for Juan would be very expensive, and that money would have to be added onto everyone's school fees, which also wouldn't be fair.

Juan seemed really disappointed and upset about this. 'I just want life to be a bit easier. Is that too much to ask?' he said. To make things worse, all his friends went out to see a movie at the end of the day, and Juan couldn't go because it wasn't in a cinema that had anywhere for him to sit.

WHAT IS THE FAIR THING TO DO HERE? IT DOES SEEM IMPORTANT THAT NOBODY GETS SPECIAL TREATMENT, BUT IT ALSO SEEMS UNFAIR THAT THE WAY SCHOOLS, TRANSPORT AND EVERYTHING ELSE HAS BEEN BUILT MAKES LIFE SO DIFFICULT FOR JUAN. IS JUAN ASKING FOR SPECIAL TREATMENT IF ALL HE WANTS IS AN ORDINARY LIFE LIKE EVERYONE ELSE?

Agent Mae signing out

INCOMING PHILOSO-MAIL

NEW MESSAGE

TO: AGENT MAE @ BRAINS TRUST

FROM: DR MATT @ SHORT & CURLY HQ

SUBJECT: DR MATT PHILOSO-MAIL

Wow! These are some BIG questions. (Get it? Big? You're not the only one who can make jokes, Mae.)

People talk about things being fair or unfair all the time, but what do these words actually mean? I hope you packed your **magnifying glass**, because we're going to start by **defining our terms**.

'What does the word **fair** mean?' I hear you say.

I'm so glad you asked! Most people think we treat people fairly when we treat them the same way we'd treat anybody else in the same situation. So if a teacher gave you a detention for fidgeting in class, but then didn't give a detention to your classmate who was fidgeting just as much, then the teacher would be treating you unfairly.

Unfortunately, treating people the same way isn't as simple as it sounds. Being fair doesn't just mean treating everyone the exact same way because people often need different things to get the same result. Therefore, fairness is about getting the same outcome, from the same situation, as much as possible.

Let's go back to Juan. Even though other students at school are able to sit in the same chairs, to treat Juan fairly, the school would have to provide him with a desk and chair big enough to meet his needs. That might be slightly inconvenient for the school, but it's a way of making sure everyone's needs are considered.

Remember how at the start of the book we said 'normal' was a boring word? Well, sometimes ideas about who and what is normal can cause ethical problems too – because there's always some group of people who get to decide what's normal and what's not, and that can lead to other people's needs being forgotten or ignored.

Plus, Juan isn't the only person who might not be 'normal' – there might be people who use wheelchairs or have back pain (so standard chairs don't suit them) and all kinds of other things. When you take a closer look, there aren't many people who are totally 'normal'!

Imagine if we didn't assume it was 'normal' to be able to hear perfectly. If this was the case, every movie at the cinema would have subtitles. Movie-goers who can hear really well might find them distracting, but maybe that would be a fair price to pay to make sure people who have trouble hearing can enjoy the films everyone else can.

But we can only take this so far. Sometimes, giving people the exact same outcome will come at a high price and would unfairly affect everybody else. For example, imagine if Juan's school had to buy a bus big enough for him to fit comfortably in: it would probably be very expensive. That money might have been spent paying for jerseys for sports teams, buying new textbooks or something else that might have been good for everybody, not just for Juan.

So how far should we go in designing a world that allows us to live the best life we can? A philosopher named **John Rawls** used a **thought experiment** to help us figure it out (get your **maps** out).

> Imagine you weren't born yet, but you could think and make decisions. You don't know what you'll be like when you're born. You might be born super tall, like Juan, average-sized, or short. Now, imagine you could write the rules for society, but you had to do it not knowing which height you would be.

What rules would you write, not knowing what height you'd be? Rawls thought whatever you came up with would be the fairest set of rules, because they'd be written with people thinking about the needs of *each* group, not just the most common or popular one.

Dr Matt signing out

THINKING QUESTIONS

1. What would society look like if it were designed with people like Juan in mind, as well as average-sized people?

2. Do you think it's fair for Juan to have the same sized desk as everyone else?

3. Should the school get a bigger bus so Juan can use it as well? If not, is it fair that Juan might have to go to school by himself instead of being with his friends?

FAIRNESS DEFINITION

When people are the same and the situation is the same, treat them the same.

When people are different or the situation is different, treat them differently (if you need to).

REMEMBER: this is a pretty hard thing to do. It's almost impossible to treat everybody the exact same way, or to know every tiny difference that might be relevant in every situation.

I'VE GOT A LOVELY BUNCH OF COCONUTS!

I think this calls for another little **thought experiment**.

Imagine we're both stuck on a desert island and we're not going to be saved for two days. We don't have much food – we only have ten coconuts to eat. To survive, I need to eat three coconuts a day, but you only need two coconuts a day because you're not as big as I am. (I've got lots more muscles, you know. Big and strong. Definitely not because I've eaten too much pizza.)

What would be the fair thing to do? Should we both get an equal number of coconuts? Should we get to keep all the coconuts we each find? Or should we divide them up based on what we both need?

YOU DECIDE! Think about what the best option would be. How would this apply to Juan's situation?

RESEARCH UPDATE

NEW MESSAGE

TO: DR MATT @ SHORT & CURLY HQ

FROM: AGENT MAE @ BRAINS TRUST

SUBJECT: RESEARCH UPDATE ON JUAN RODRIGUEZ

Today, Juan's school is having their athletics carnival. Most people have trained pretty hard, but a few of the school's top athletes aren't even going to bother competing.

One of them said to me, 'What's the point? Juan is going to win everything. His giant long legs make him unbeatable. Long distance, sprinting, long jump, high jump – we just can't beat him, so why bother trying? It's so unfair.'

It turns out, he was right. Juan won, and set a new record, in every event he entered. Those long legs really paid off. You might even say they were LEGendary. Get it? Look out jokesters, there's a new queen in town!

There are also rumours Juan is going to get signed to a big AFL team as well. Pretty cool, right? He'll be a professional athlete before he even finishes school. Lots of his classmates are pretty jealous, but Juan says he'd much rather be normal.

'They can have my records and sports contracts. I just want to be able to hang out with my friends, go to the movies, have a sleepover – you know, normal kid stuff.'

His wish might come true. Apparently, some scientists have come up with a painless way to make Juan shorter. They've invented a special medicine, which is supposed to taste like Vegemite, brussels sprouts and caramel ice cream mixed together (yuck!) and would make him average-sized. The scientist in charge told me that this is the best chance Juan has of being 'normal'.

Juan can see how this drug might let him live an ordinary life, but he's really unsure. He feels weird at the thought of having to change who he is just to get by in society. Juan's parents don't like the idea of the 'medicine'. They said, 'Who says Juan isn't normal already? Why should he have to change so that he can fit in? Maybe it's the world that needs to change. There's nothing wrong with our son!'

I'M NOT SURE IF JUAN SHOULD CHANGE OR NOT. IT'S A TRICKY SITUATION. ON THE ONE HAND, I WOULDN'T WANT TO MISS OUT ON BEING WITH MY FRIENDS, BUT ON THE OTHER I'D ALSO FIND IT REALLY HARD TO WALK AWAY FROM A CAREER AS AN AFL STAR! WHAT SHOULD JUAN DO?

Agent Mae signing out

INCOMING PHILOSO-MAIL

NEW MESSAGE

TO: AGENT MAE @ BRAINS TRUST
FROM: DR MATT @ SHORT & CURLY HQ
SUBJECT: DR MATT PHILOSO-MAIL

I'm a bit jealous of Juan now! The only athletics awards I ever won at school were third-place ribbons. And that's only because there were three people in the race. So I can see why it would be confusing to hear he wants to change back to have an average-sized body.

To get to the bottom of this, I think we need to get our **torches** out and look at Juan with some **curiosity and empathy**. True, it might be awesome to win some ribbons one day a year at the athletics carnival, but he's then got to get in his expensive, custom-made car to go home to his giant, custom-made bed. If he wants to hang out with his friends, he has to hope they'll go somewhere he can fit comfortably, and not many places seem very Juan-friendly. So even though the advantages of his life sound pretty good to us, the disadvantages might not seem worth it to him. Also, it's his life to live, so we should be careful about criticising his decision.

Still, I've got a few questions about the scientists who designed the so-called 'cure' for being tall. Have you ever heard of a cure for being brown-eyed? Or for being left-handed? How about a medicine used to treat people who like cats more than dogs? Of course not! They don't have anything that needs curing (OK, maybe the people who like cats more are a bit nutty, but besides that . . .).

For the scientists to come up with a way to 'fix' Juan, there would have to be something wrong with him in the first place. But is there?

The scientists said they would help Juan to be 'normal', but that's a word we need to look at closely. Whenever someone talks about what's 'normal', we should be on full alert because we'll probably need to **test some assumptions** about what's normal. In this case, the scientists are assuming that being tall is a bad thing just because it's not 'normal'.

Let's take a closer look at Juan's situation, being tall in a world designed for average-sized people is a kind of disability. It's a bit like being in a wheelchair in a world designed for people who can walk. I wonder if we could **find some similarities** that might be helpful.

People who think about ethics and disability talk a lot about **ableism.** Ableism is when we assume it's better for people to have average bodies (without disabilities) and only see the world from the perspective of an able-bodied person. Some people think it's a problem because it assumes disability is a bad thing and that it's better to be 'normal'.

In response to ableism, we might ask what's so great about being normal? Is it that there's something special about 'normal' bodies? Or has the world been designed to suit people with average bodies, and that gives them an advantage?

Unless we've experienced what the world is like from someone else's perspective, it's pretty hard to know. That's why we need to listen to people like Juan and take their opinion seriously, even if we think we'd want to keep being tall if we were in his enormous, gigantic shoes. It might make us wonder who got to decide who was 'normal'? At some stage in our lives, lots of us will be 'abnormal' in some way – we might be injured, elderly or develop an illness. Does the idea of 'normal' need to **check it's assumptions** about the variety of different body types humans can have?

Some people assume it would be bad to be deaf, blind, have to live in a wheelchair, or (in Juan's case) be really tall, but *why* is it bad? Maybe it's partly because the world wasn't built for people who can't see, hear, walk or fit underneath a two-metre door. Imagine if we built the world we were talking about in **John Rawls' thought experiment**, would we still think it was bad to be tall?

Dr Matt signing out

THINKING QUESTIONS

1. Do you think there is such a thing as a normal person? What are they like?

2. If you were in Juan's shoes, would you have taken the cure?

FUN FACTS: IT'S GOOD TO BE TALL

Researchers have found tall people (but not as tall as Juan) actually have it pretty good. Tall people often:

- Get treated like they're leaders by the people around them.
- Tend to earn more money than short people.
- Are more likely to be happy with their lives than their shorter buddies.

This is why it's so important to use our **hiking poles** to **check our assumptions** and **question our emotions**. Just because we feel like taller people are smarter or more inspiring doesn't mean they are. If we don't **check our assumptions**, we might be being unfair to all the awesome shorties in the world!

We should also do some **fact finding** to see whether everything about being tall is so great. Turns out, it might not be so peachy. Tall people often:

- Find it hard to find clothes that fit.
- Get cramped more easily when sitting on buses, planes and other kinds of transport.
- Are more likely to die earlier than short people (oh, that's depressing).

Maybe I wouldn't want to be tall after all?

AGENT DEBRIEF

NEW MESSAGE

TO: DR MATT @ SHORT & CURLY HQ
FROM: AGENT MAE @ BRAINS TRUST
SUBJECT: AGENT MAE – DEBRIEF FOR HQ

The more I think about Juan, the more I realise his situation isn't actually unique. Lots of people find it hard to live in society because they are different. Maybe they need a wheelchair – like Arjun – or maybe they have an illness that means they have to miss lots of days of school. Just like Juan, they'd need to be treated differently to have the same chances as the rest of us. I guess we could say fairness isn't about treating everyone the same, it's about treating people based on what they need.

Juan still has heaps of really cool skills. It's not like he can't do awesome stuff. So we would need to be careful not to give people different treatment unless they need it, right? Like, I know Arjun is in a wheelchair, but he can still kick my butt at tennis, so it wouldn't be fair to give him more advantages in a match, would it?

That's it! I've decided Arjun has to play left-handed next time we play tennis. Using his opposite hand will finally give me a chance at winning!

Agent Mae signing out

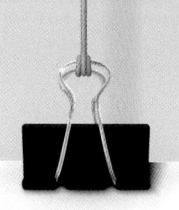

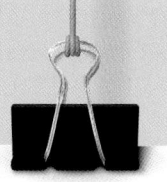

TRENDS

THE BEST SHOP
BUY TODAY, CHUCK IT TOMORROW!

WHAT'S THE DEAL WITH STICK-Os?

MIA WONG

FIELD RESEARCH REPORT:

SUBJECT: Mia Wong

DETAILS: The only kid in school without a Stick-O.

NOTES:

- Should we buy things that are bad for the environment?
- Why are we so obsessed with stuff?
- What is the point of toys?

AGENT SOPHIA

REPORT RUN-DOWN

NEW MESSAGE

TO: DR MATT @ SHORT & CURLY HQ
FROM: AGENT SOPHIA @ BRAINS TRUST
SUBJECT: REPORT RUN-DOWN ON MIA WONG

During a routine patrol, I came across the most amazing sight. I saw a school lit up like a rainbow. There were lights flashing, bright colours and creative, happy students everywhere. It was AMAZING! I just had to have a look. It was a bit like those bug zappers that draw in insects and then kill them, except luckily, I'm still alive (phew).

Everywhere I look there are students running around and having the most wonderful time. Some have made cubbyhouses and set up forts. Others are having realistic lightsaber duels with lit-up sticks – it's like magic! If I had some of these amazing sticks I'd build my own awesome animal park. It would be so spectacular and glow so bright you would be able to see it from space! I reckon it would even secure a spot on the wonders of the world list . . .

Anyway – these fancy sticks. They're so cool, except for one thing. They're pretty fragile. Any kicks or bumps usually break them. After that, they get thrown in the bin and the kid who owned it starts crying.

It turns out these sticks aren't magic at all. They're a new toy everyone is buying called 'Stick-Os'. All the ads say, 'Just like sticks, only better'.

Not all of the kids are loving these brilliant sticks. One student, called Mia Wong, is asking the teachers to ban Stick-Os from the school. She says Stick-Os are bad for the environment. The factories overseas where they're made need a lot of power to run, which creates pollution. Also, when the Stick-Os break they can't be recycled, they just end up as more rubbish.

Agent Sophia signing out

THE SCHOOL LOOKS SO BEAUTIFUL THOUGH, AND STICK-OS LOOK FUN! DOES IT REALLY MATTER IF THEY GET CHUCKED IN THE BIN AT THE END OF THE DAY?

INCOMING PHILOSO-MAIL

NEW MESSAGE

TO: AGENT SOPHIA @ BRAINS TRUST
FROM: DR MATT @ SHORT & CURLY HQ
SUBJECT: DR MATT PHILOSO-MAIL

Before I answer your question, let me ask you one . . . What's the biggest animal in the world?

It's the blue whale, weighing a massive 140,000 kilograms (that's 140 tonnes). African bush elephants are the biggest land-based animal. They weigh as much as 10 tonnes. Now, imagine how much space you'd need to fit 457 blue whales in a room together. Or maybe you'd prefer to squeeze roughly 6400 elephants into that room.

Why am I making you imagine this? Because that's basically how much rubbish Australia produces each year. The last time someone recorded our waste output (in 2016), Australia produced about 64 million tonnes of rubbish. More than half was recycled, which is good, but that still leaves approximately 25 million tonnes of rubbish that needs to go somewhere. And that somewhere is called landfill. That's right, we fill the land with rubbish! Some people are worried we don't have enough landfill sites available.

Creating more landfill sites may not be a solution. All landfill has a bunch of knock-on effects on the environment and the natural habitats of wildlife. Usually, if something affects the environment it'll end up affecting our health too.

When someone chucks out a broken Stick-O, it doesn't

magically disappear. It keeps taking up valuable space on the planet. When we run out of space – and we will at the current rate – people and animals will probably suffer. It's important to know this, because it's so easy to throw something in the bin and forget about it. It disappears into the rubbish truck and we never have to see it again, but that's not how rubbish works.

Of course, this doesn't mean we can't do *anything* that creates rubbish. That would be basically impossible! What it does mean is we need to take responsibility for the mess we make. We need to be aware of how our actions affect the environment. If we care about looking after the planet, we should try to leave as little mess behind as we can.

Let's look at these Stick-Os. They're pretty much sticks, except colourful. They don't let you do anything you couldn't do with an ordinary stick; they just let you do it in a way that looks a bit cooler. But in exchange for that *tiny* boost in fun, there's a *giant* impact on the planet. Does that seem like a fair trade?

Dr Matt signing out

THINKING QUESTIONS

1. What would you give up or do less often to make sure you weren't leaving as much rubbish in the world?

2. Has your school had any 'crazes'? Did you want to be part of them? Why?

3. How can you tell whether a new craze at school is going to last?

AUSTRALIA'S RUBBISH AS ANIMALS

If we had a set of scales with all of Australia's rubbish on one side, here's what we would need to balance the scales.

- 457 blue whales
- 6400 African bull elephants
- 28,000 white rhinos
- 556,000 giant pandas
- 750,000 adult humans
- 2.4 million wombats
- 85 million meerkats
- 1.25 billion goldfish

RESEARCH UPDATE

NEW MESSAGE	

TO: DR MATT @ SHORT & CURLY HQ

FROM: AGENT SOPHIA @ BRAINS TRUST

SUBJECT: RESEARCH UPDATE ON MIA WONG

Good news for all the Stick-O fans out there – the teachers didn't ban them!

Not such good news for Mia. She's still refusing to play with them. She's got an ordinary stick. Actually, it's a pretty good one – solid, good length, smooth. She wants to join in and play swordfights with a group of students who are pretending to be pirates with their Stick-O laser swords, but they won't let her play. They say her stick is boring and won't be as fun.

'Cool kids only, sorry!' one of them yelled to her as she walked away.

Poor Mia! All she wants to do is play.

WHY DOES IT MATTER WHETHER MIA HAS A STICK-O? CAN THE STUFF YOU OWN REALLY MAKE YOU COOLER? ARE YOU UNCOOL IF YOU DON'T HAVE THE THINGS EVERYONE ELSE HAS?

Agent Sophia signing out

INCOMING PHILOSO-MAIL

NEW MESSAGE

TO: AGENT SOPHIA @ BRAINS TRUST

FROM: DR MATT @ SHORT & CURLY HQ

SUBJECT: DR MATT PHILOSO-MAIL

One of the main reasons lots of school fads get banned is because there will always be some students who get left out. Not everybody is allowed to buy certain toys – and not everyone can afford them. If you have to have a Stick-O in order to have friends, then that seems unfair on people who don't have them or don't want them.

We've learned something important by seeing the way Mia's been treated. Once toys like Stick-Os start becoming popular, people don't want it because it's a fun toy, they want it because they want to be cool (or at least, that's part of the reason). They want to be part of the thing everyone else is doing. That way, they feel like they belong.

Humans have always lived in communities. We work together, spend time with each other and need the help of other people to be healthy and happy. This means we're scared of being left out or being abandoned. One way of making sure we're never going to be left behind is by trying to do whatever the most popular and powerful people are doing – we wear the same clothes, buy the same toys.

'Cool' is a fancy way of talking about the things that make us feel included. There's nothing wrong with wanting to be included, but we should be careful not to spend all our time trying to be cool, because what's cool inevitably changes. Stick-Os won't always be cool; soon it will be something else.

If we spend all our time trying to be cool and imitate other people, it's hard to find out who we really are. Philosophers call this **authenticity** – when we live the way we want to live, no matter what other people are doing. Mia might not be 'cool' according to the other kids, but she's being authentic, and that's extremely special in its own way.

People with authenticity know what they believe in, what makes them happy and how they want to live. People who just want to be cool are always looking to someone else for answers, which can be confusing, frustrating and even lonely.

That doesn't mean everyone who buys a Stick-O isn't authentic or just wants to fit in, but we need to pay attention to why we're doing what we're doing. Are we buying a toy because we think it will be a fun game, or are we doing it just because everyone else is?

If we're doing it because we're trying to fit in, we should do our best to remember one of the most important points in ethics: YOU matter. You don't matter because of what you do or what you own; you matter because of who you are. You're a person, and that makes you special. Lots of philosophers call this **dignity** – and because you have dignity, you don't need to own stuff in order to be valued.

Dr Matt signing out

THE MUSEUM OF CRAZES

Has a new craze hit your school? Maybe some of them have come into fashion more than once! Here are a bunch of fads that have popped up over the years. If you don't know what they are, go ask someone who was at school at the time. They'll definitely know!

1950s — Knucklebones, Marbles

1960s — Action man, conkers

1970s — Trolls

1980s — slinkies, yo-yos, Rubik's cubes, Football cards

1990s — Tamagotchi, Diablos

2000s — Gameboy, Pokémon

2010s — fidget spinners, Slime

110

A PHILOSOPHER'S GUIDE TO TOY SHOPPING

Here are some simple questions you can ask yourself to work out whether you should buy that toy:

- Would you want to buy it if you weren't allowed to tell anyone you owned it?
- Does it make your life more fun?
- Is there a less fancy version you could have just as much fun with?
- Can you recycle it?
- If it breaks, can you fix it?
- Will other people be able to play with you if they don't have the toy?

It's OK to say no to some of these questions, but make sure you know *why* you want to buy something, and then make sure those reasons are good ones. Remember, our **hiking poles** are for **questioning our emotions**. **Desire** is an emotion and it tells us we want something, but we should be curious: why do we want this? Do we really need it?

THE HAPPINESS TREADMILL

You know the old saying 'money can't buy you happiness'? It's not entirely true. When you buy something new, it does make you happy for a little while, but often the happiness fades. You get used to the new thing and you need to get something else to feel another happiness boost. This means we're stuck on a treadmill, constantly chasing the next 'thing' that might make us happy.

AGENT DEBRIEF

NEW MESSAGE

TO: DR MATT @ SHORT & CURLY HQ
FROM: AGENT SOPHIA @ BRAINS TRUST
SUBJECT: AGENT SOPHIA – DEBRIEF FOR HQ

As I sit here, playing with a Stick-O one of the students gave me, I can't help but feel that all this worry about the world is getting in the way of us having fun. Who wants to be the party pooper when everybody's having a good time?

However, from what I can tell, we're not doing enough to look after the environment. Plus, the people and animals that are being most affected by pollution aren't the ones who get to play with Stick-Os. That doesn't seem fair – and when I know all this, playing with Stick-Os doesn't seem fun anymore. So maybe Mia is on to something? And seeing as nobody likes a party pooper, Mia's pretty brave by standing up for her beliefs.

Still, is it really up to kids to change the planet? Aren't there other things we can do to stop pollution instead of taking away all the fun stuff?

I guess what I'm saying is, I'm going to keep the Stick-O, but I don't want Earth to end up being the messiest planet in the universe, so I'm also going to make my whole family recycle more. That's a good deal, right?

Agent Sophia signing out

PROMISES

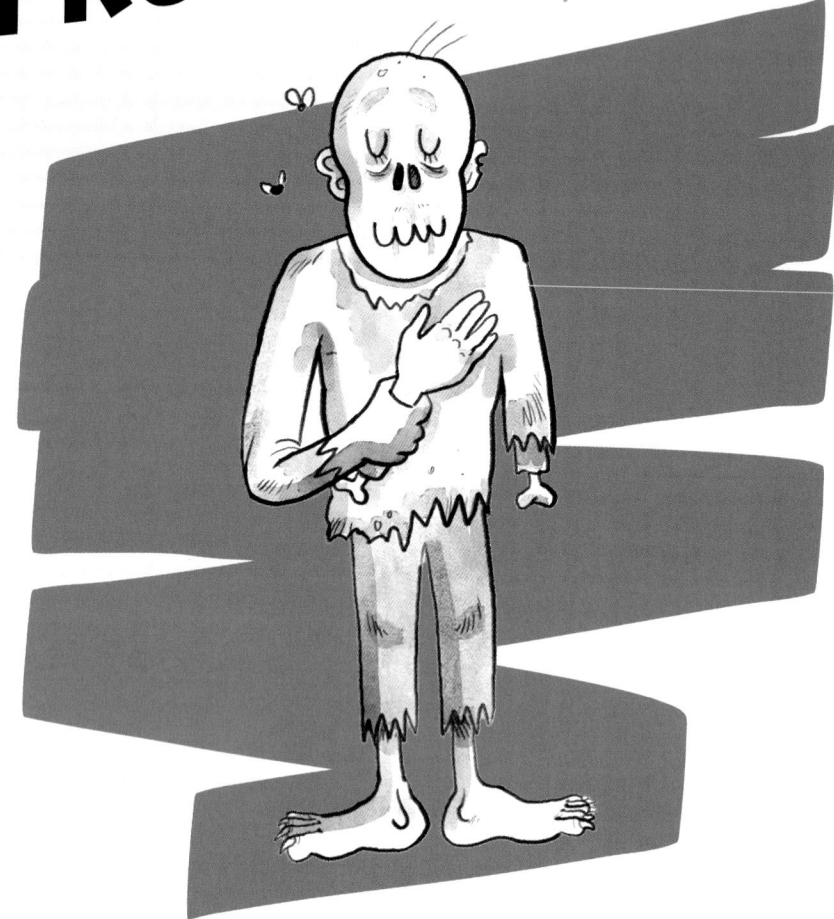

END OF DAYS 4: ZOMBIE SURVIVAL ETHICS

SKYLAR DOTSON

FIELD RESEARCH REPORT:

SUBJECT: Skylar Dotson

DETAILS: Avid video gamer.

NOTES:

- Should we always keep our promises?
- Does it matter if we do the wrong thing in a video game?

AGENT KOA

REPORT RUN-DOWN

NEW MESSAGE

TO: DR MATT @ SHORT & CURLY HQ

FROM: AGENT KOA @ BRAINS TRUST

SUBJECT: REPORT RUN-DOWN ON SKYLAR DOTSON

Skylar is a very excited puppy right now. She's finally got her hands on *End of Days 4*. It's a game where the world has been taken over by zombies and demons and nearly every human is dead. (It's awesome — I've got a copy back at HQ. Make sure the others don't play it without me — I'm up to a good spot!) You play with a team of other survivors. They're computer characters, not real people, but that hasn't stopped Skylar from getting attached to them. She likes a lot of the characters she is teamed up with, which seems weird to me. How can you be friends with a computer? I've played stacks of games and never become attached to the characters.

Anyway, Skylar's been playing this game all day and she's been doing really well. Until now. Two of the people in her team are surrounded by zombies and they need her help, but she won't have time to save them both. Skylar has to pick between Amara, who is a great fighter, can pick locks (which is very useful) and has a family back at base camp, and Bill, who doesn't have any special skills and is a bit of a grumpy old guy.

Actually, Bill kind of reminds me of my grandpa. He was a grumpy old bloke on the outside, but was nice in his own way. He just didn't always show how much he cared about people. I wonder if Bill's a big softie on the inside. I'm worried about what Skylar's going to do now.

Skylar has paused the game to call her friend, who is also a gamer. She explains that she wants to save Amara because she's more helpful to the team and is more likely to save other team members lives later on in the game. Plus, Skylar likes her better and she's got a family. Decision made! Here's the catch — Bill.

The only reason Bill is part of Skylar's team is because she promised to keep him safe. Earlier in the game, Bill wasn't even part of the team.

Skylar started talking to him anyway and he told her he wanted to help her team, but he was scared of dying. Skylar PROMISED to make sure nothing bad would happen to him, and that's why he joined the team.

WHAT A SUCKY SITUATION! SKYLAR HAS TO CHOOSE BETWEEN PROTECTING THE PERSON SHE THINKS DESERVES PROTECTING AND THE PERSON SHE PROMISED TO PROTECT. IT'S A TOUGH ONE. BILL IS A BIT OF A GRUMP AND AMARA IS A REALLY TOUGH FIGHTER, BUT A PROMISE IS A PROMISE, RIGHT?

Agent Koa signing out

INCOMING PHILOSO-MAIL

NEW MESSAGE

TO: AGENT KOA @ BRAINS TRUST
FROM: DR MATT @ SHORT & CURLY HQ
SUBJECT: DR MATT PHILOSO-MAIL

Zombies, demons, promises, ethics . . . OH MY! Is it my birthday? This is so exciting!

Promises are funny things, aren't they, Koa? They're almost magical. When we say 'I promise', we create an **obligation**, which is something we *have* to do. It would be wrong if we didn't. Now, obligations aren't that special; we have heaps of them: not to kill people, not to lie to them or steal their sandwiches (unless it's Nutella, obviously). We don't choose these obligations, we just have them. When we make a promise, we create a brand-new, shiny obligation, which I think is pretty cool.

If we think of a promise as just like any other obligation, it means it's wrong if we don't keep our promise. That's tricky because Skylar wants to leave Bill to die even though she promised to save him. Poor, grumpy, soon-to-be-dead Bill. (Wait, will Bill come back as a zombie and want revenge? I want to play this game now. Did you say we had a copy here at HQ? Awesome . . .)

Most people think promises are super important, but there might be extreme situations where it would be all right to break a promise. For example, if Bill started to attack Skylar, then she would be allowed to break her promise to keep him safe in order to save her own life. Her obligation to keep herself alive is more important than the promise. I think we need to **make some distinctions** between the different reasons *why* Skylar wants to break her promise to Bill. **Machetes** at the ready everyone (we might need them with all these zombies around).

From the research report, I can see three reasons why Skylar would want to save Amara instead of Bill:

- Amara is more useful to the team.
- Amara has a cute little family.
- Bill is a big grumblebum.

The question is, are any of these reasons more important than the promise? One way to think about this is to imagine what Skylar would say to Bill before she let him die. If she said, 'Sorry, Bill, I just like Amara better than you, so I'm gonna save her,' he'd think she was totally heartless (and he'd probably be right)! On the other hand, if Skylar said, 'Sorry, Bill, I have an obligation to keep everyone on the team alive, and Amara is more likely to help keep our team safe in the future,' then that's a more reasonable argument. So one of the things that matters is *why* Skylar wants to pick Amara.

OK, I'm with you, Koa. I'm starting to feel really bad for Bill now. SAVE BILL, SKYLAR!

There's another lesson here: we need to be very careful about the promises we make. Sometimes we make promises that are impossible to keep, and that's an ethical problem because it gets us into situations like this one, where we're stuck. Skylar probably should never have promised that nothing would ever happen to Bill, because that's not a promise she could keep. After all, it's a world of zombies and demons! Nobody is safe. Not even you . . .

MUAHAHAHAHAHAHAHAHAHA

(Sorry, I've been practising my evil laugh. What do you think?)

Dr Matt signing out

THINKING QUESTIONS

1. Do you think it's OK to break a promise if it's too hard to keep?

2. What would you do if you'd made a promise you shouldn't have made, like Skylar did?

3. Would you keep your promise to Bill, or save Amara?

PROMISES AND ICE CREAM

The German philosopher **Immanuel Kant** wrote a lot about promises. He was also a pretty strict chap (he was well-known for taking his afternoon walk at EXACTLY the same time every day – people even joked they could set their watch by his schedule). Kant said it was always wrong to break a promise and he had a really interesting reason for saying so.

Kant thought part of being ethical was being consistent, so if we thought it was OK for us to do something, it would have to be OK for everyone else to do it. If it's OK for us to break promises, it should be OK for everyone to break promises. This puts promise-breakers in a bit of a pickle.

Why? Imagine a world where everyone was allowed to break their promises. Would you ever believe somebody when they said 'I promise' if you knew they could easily break that promise later? Of course not. It would be MAYHEM! I could promise to pay you for a delicious ice cream and then run away and never come back. And because you'd know I was probably going to break my promise, you'd never give me the ice cream in the first place.

A world without ice cream? Madness, I tell you!

RESEARCH UPDATE

NEW MESSAGE

TO: DR MATT @ SHORT & CURLY HQ
FROM: AGENT KOA @ BRAINS TRUST
SUBJECT: RESEARCH UPDATE ON SKYLAR DOTSON

I don't believe it. Bill's dead! Skylar broke her promise. The good news is that Amara's alive and she's awesome: picking locks and kicking butt. Plus, another member of Amara's family even joined Skylar's team because she saved her life! I guess she made the right decision.

Skylar called her friend back to discuss the game. They started talking about Bill. Skylar's friend reckons Bill dying doesn't really matter because it's just a video game. She said, 'Who cares if we do the wrong thing when it's just a game with made-up people? There are games out there that let you shoot innocent people on the street, run them over in your car and all kinds of horrible stuff, but it's just fun. It's not like you actually let someone die. There's no right or wrong in video games.'

Skylar doesn't agree though. She feels pretty guilty about it all. She asked, 'I still broke my promise, doesn't that make me a bad person?' (I think so. Poor, tough-on-the-outside-but-sweet-on-the-inside Bill. I miss him already. SHAME ON YOU, SKYLAR.) Skylar's friend wasn't budging, but still, Skylar couldn't stop thinking about this and said to her friend, 'If I wouldn't break a promise in real life, why is it OK in a video game?'

WHO IS RIGHT – SKYLAR OR HER FRIEND? HELP ME OUT! ARE THERE ANY ETHICS IN VIDEO GAMES?

Agent Koa signing out

INCOMING PHILOSO-MAIL

NEW MESSAGE

TO: AGENT KOA @ BRAINS TRUST
FROM: DR MATT @ SHORT & CURLY HQ
SUBJECT: DR MATT PHILOSO-MAIL

Oh no! RIP, Bill, forever in our hearts.

Koa, you've asked a really interesting question. And as a gamer, it's one I think you'd be keen to figure out. In order to answer this curly question – you guessed it – we're going to need to **make some distinctions!**

First, what does **unethical** mean? It can mean a few different things.

Some people think something is unethical when it hurts somebody. If that's the case, then it seems harsh to say we can do the wrong thing playing a video game. You can't hurt a computer character – they're just little bits of code popping up on the screen. So if we think unethical actions are ones that are bad for other people, then it might be impossible to hurt a video game.

We can also say things are unethical because they are bad for us. Some things are bad because they do bad things to our character. When we're rude, lazy, selfish or whatever, it's not just bad because it hurts someone else, it's bad because it makes us a worse sort of person.

An ancient Greek philosopher named **Aristotle** thought ethics was basically about becoming a good person – someone who had lots of **virtues**. Virtues are parts of our character that help us do what's right and avoid what's wrong – you know, stuff like kindness, honesty, courage, generosity and self-control. The way we get these virtues is by doing virtuous things, which is pretty obvious really. If you want to be an honest person, do lots of honest things! And vice versa, if you do nasty things, you'll become a nasty person. This would suggest, in Skylar's situation, she might want to worry whether breaking her promise to Bill makes her a less trustworthy person, even if it is just in a video game.

On the flip side, it might sometimes be a really good idea to do the wrong thing in a video game. When studying ethics, we want to *understand* as much as we can about good and bad, right and wrong. The problem is, we can't learn about doing the wrong thing in the real world because we might hurt somebody! That's where stuff like books and movies can be useful. We watch things happen on screen and we react emotionally to them, which we can learn from and apply to real life.

This is why Aristotle thought the theatre was a good environment to practise and learn about ethics. If Aristotle were alive today, I think he'd probably say the same thing about video games – maybe he'd even be a game designer!

So Skylar now has the chance to learn what it feels like to break a promise. What were the consequences? Did her teammates judge her?

These are real-life questions, but we might be able to work them out in a make-believe world. And Skylar did feel guilty for breaking her promise to Bill, which gives her something to think about next time she makes a real-world promise.

(That's a fancy way of saying, 'It's OK to binge on computer games sometimes' – go on, show this to your parents the next time they say you've played enough for one day!)

Dr Matt signing out

THINKING QUESTIONS

1. Have you ever done the wrong thing to a fictional or imaginary character in a game? How did it make you feel?

2. Is it OK to do bad things in video games, like kill, lie or steal?

FUN FACTS: PINKY PROMISES

Have you ever made a pinky promise? Two people lock their pinky fingers together and make a promise, which is somehow made stronger because the pinkies are involved. Who said pinkies were the weakest finger? Most people see it as a 'super promise', a bit like the Unbreakable Vow in Harry Potter: if you break it, you die. (OK, FINE, we don't actually die if we break a pinky promise, but it's seen as being extra bad.)

The pinky promise originated in Japan, where it's called *yubikiri*. Apparently, people would make a pinky promise and recite a little poem, which basically says, 'The person who breaks this promise has to cut off their finger, receive 10,000 punches and swallow 1000 needles'. Holy cow! That's a pretty nasty fate for breaking a promise. Where do you even get 1000 needles from? It sounds like a lot of work; I'm tired just thinking about it.

Today, you're not likely to have to swallow a bunch of sewing needles if you break a promise, but the idea of this pinky promise is still around. In Japan, people still say *'yubikiri'* when they make promises, and all around the world people think pinky promises are extra important. But don't make one unless you're OK with having your finger chopped off!

AGENT DEBRIEF

NEW MESSAGE
TO: DR MATT @ SHORT & CURLY HQ
FROM: AGENT KOA @ BRAINS TRUST
SUBJECT: AGENT KOA – DEBRIEF FOR HQ

I wonder if Skylar would have broken her promise if Bill had been a real person instead of a video-game character.

This got me thinking about the time I was taking care of my cousin's pet dog. I promised the dog we'd go for walks every day, but it rained most of the time we had him at our house, so some days we just stayed indoors. I don't think I broke a promise, because the dog didn't understand the promise I was making. Perhaps it's the same with video games? It didn't matter that Skylar broke her promise to Bill because he never understood it in the first place.

Skylar is going to have to make lots of promises throughout her life. Adults make promises all the time: when they get married, they promise to tell the truth in court; even fancy legal contracts are basically promises that get written down. But because she's making those promises to real people, I wonder if she'll be more likely to keep her word?

Now, kick everyone else out of the games room. I'm almost back at HQ and I'm DESPERATE to fight some zombies!

Agent Koa signing out

FRIENDSHIP

PUTT PUTT PARTY PICKLE

ZOLA REEVE AND LOUIS FREEMAN

FIELD RESEARCH REPORT:

AGENT ARJUN

SUBJECT: Zola Reeve and Louis Freeman

DETAILS: Zola has been planning her birthday party for months, but the new kid, Louis, might change everything.

NOTES:

- Do we have to be friends with people?
- What's so good about having friends?
- Do friends have to agree with each other?

REPORT RUN-DOWN

NEW MESSAGE

TO: DR MATT @ SHORT & CURLY HQ

FROM: AGENT ARJUN @ BRAINS TRUST

SUBJECT: REPORT RUN-DOWN ON ZOLA REEVE AND LOUIS FREEMAN

I know my next mission isn't meant to start for a couple of days, but I signed on because I'm extremely dedicated and professional; it had nothing to do with the fact I'm pretty excited. I've been assigned to observe Zola Reeve and her friends at her birthday party on Saturday. She's been planning this party for months and she can't wait. And neither can I! The party is at Do-nut Putt Putt, a donut-themed Putt Putt course — how awesome is that! Instead of putting the ball into a hole, you putt it into the middle of a donut. Genius, huh? Plus, they have a FREE DONUT BAR!

Food, sport and friends? It's my dream come true (even if I'm just an observer).

Speaking of friends though, there has been one downside to this assignment. The other day, while I was in ultimate field research mode, making notes on Zola and her friends at school, I suddenly noticed a boy sitting all by himself. I couldn't work out why he looked so sad and lonely — so I did a little digging. Turns out his name is Louis and he's a new boy in Zola's class. No one knows much about him because no one has bothered to talk to him — poor Louis!

Since then I've been keeping an eye on him. I don't think Louis has made any friends. At recess and lunch, while everyone is playing and talking, he sits by himself. Sometimes he'll bring a book to read, but a lot of the time he's just watching everyone else playing. I know I can't compromise my research by getting involved, but I really want to go and sit with him so he has someone to hang out with.

Yesterday someone finally noticed Louis' situation. Zola's older brother, Van, saw Louis looking lonely and went over to speak to him before class. Louis' face lit up at having someone to talk to. It was like seeing a totally different person! Van seems to think Louis is a cool kid.

It's all got pretty tricky though. At recess, Van suggested Zola invite Louis to her birthday party at the weekend. He thinks it would be a nice thing to do, and that Louis could use some friends.

'But I don't need any new friends,' Zola said. 'I just want to spend the day with my besties. It'll be weird and awkward to have someone I don't know coming along. Plus, there are lots of people I didn't invite to the party. It might hurt their feelings if they found out I'd invited Louis,' she added.

Van wasn't convinced. He told Zola that nice people always try to make new friends – especially with people who are new to a place. He thinks, if Zola wants to be a nice person, she should invite Louis to the party.

I'M FINDING THIS WHOLE SITUATION SUPER AWKWARD. I KIND OF AGREE WITH VAN, BUT HE WAS A BIT HARSH TO ZOLA AS WELL. DOES SHE HAVE TO BECOME FRIENDS WITH LOUIS JUST BECAUSE HE'S LONELY? ISN'T IT OK FOR HER TO WANT TO TREAT HER FRIENDS DIFFERENTLY AND ONLY SPEND TIME WITH THEM, ESPECIALLY ON HER BIRTHDAY?

Agent Arjun signing out

INCOMING PHILOSO-MAIL

NEW MESSAGE

TO: AGENT ARJUN @ BRAINS TRUST
FROM: DR MATT @ SHORT & CURLY HQ
SUBJECT: DR MATT PHILOSO-MAIL

Have you ever heard of the Narnia books, Arjun? You should check them out. It's a fantasy series by an author named **C. S. Lewis**, who was awesome. He wasn't just a fiction writer, he was a really deep thinker and philosopher as well.

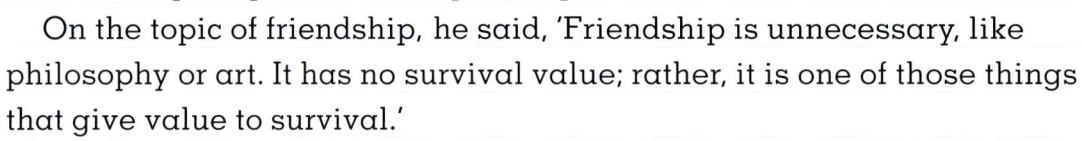

On the topic of friendship, he said, 'Friendship is unnecessary, like philosophy or art. It has no survival value; rather, it is one of those things that give value to survival.'

That's a fancy way of saying even though we don't *need* friendship in order to stay alive, if we didn't have friendship, we'd have one less reason to keep on living. We don't have to agree with Lewis, but his point is still worth thinking about. Friendship is one of the major ways we find meaning in our lives – and it's obviously upsetting for Louis that he doesn't have any friends.

Back to your other question – does that mean Zola *has* to become his friend? I don't think so. For one thing, we can't force someone to become friends with us, nor can we force ourselves to become friends with somebody else. To figure this out, you know what we need to do, right? We need to **define our terms** – **magnifying glasses** out, everyone! To become a friend, we need a few things.

1. We need to **choose** to be their friend at the same time they choose to be our friend.

2. To be considered friends, they also need to **care about one another** in a special way.

A philosopher named **Elizabeth Telfer** thinks affection is a crucial part of friendship. Two people might say they're friends (maybe they're Facebook friends), but if they don't actually *like* each other, then there would be something missing from their friendship.

This is important because we can't necessarily choose who we like and don't like. It's a question of how well two personalities fit together – like puzzle pieces. If two people don't fit well, no matter how much they *want* to be friends, it probably won't be possible.

Just because Zola can't force herself to become Louis' friend doesn't mean she can't try. She won't know if she wants to become his friend unless she makes an effort to get to know him. That means she should be friendly towards him even if they aren't friends yet. From the sound of things, Zola hasn't even talked to Louis in the playground, so there might be some things she can do, even if she doesn't want to invite him to her party.

You said Van was a bit harsh on Zola, but there might be some truth to what he said. If we think it's important to be a good person, then maybe part of achieving this is to always be friendly, which means acting in ways that allow friendships to form if the right personalities fit together.

It is helpful to remember that friendships can't be one-sided. If it's true that Zola needs to start being open to making new friends, then we would have to say the same for Louis as well. It can be scary being the new kid at school, and it can be hard to meet new people and try to make friends, but Louis has to show people he *wants* friends. He might need to start a conversation with someone, or ask if he can join in with someone else's game. That's easy to say, but hard to do.

It's hard for Zola as well – meeting someone for the first time can be awkward and a little bit scary. That's why we should always try to be friendly – smile, get to know the other person, ask questions and look for reasons to get along. Everyone finds it hard, but everyone also needs friends.

Dr Matt signing out

THINKING QUESTIONS

1. What do you think makes someone a good friend?

2. Have you ever had to make new friends? What were some tricks that made it easier?

3. Do you think Zola should invite Louis to her party?

ARISTOTLE'S THREE LEVELS OF FRIENDSHIP

Aristotle thought there were lots of different kinds of friendships, and lots of people still accept his **distinctions** today. He broke it down to three kinds of friends:

- **Utility friends:** 'Utility' is another word for 'useful'. Aristotle thought the lowest level of friendship was the kind of relationship you have with someone because they are useful to you in some way. They might give you something you like (maybe they've got a swimming pool and so you like getting invited to their house) or they might make you feel good, but you're only interested in them so long as they keep making you happy.

- **Pleasure friends:** Some kinds of friendship are fun. You like the other person, you enjoy their company and want to spend time together, but you don't know them very well. Aristotle called these friendships 'pleasure friendships', and he thought they were a pretty good way for two people to get along with one another. The problem, Aristotle thought, is that some people give us pleasure for the wrong reasons. We might find someone really funny or good company even though they're a bad influence on us.

- **True friends:** According to Aristotle, the best kind of friendships are those that are about *goodness* and recognising the goodness in the other person. He called these 'true friendships'. True friends care deeply about the other person and are never fully happy unless the other person is happy too. True friends don't necessarily need to spend heaps of time together (although it helps), because their friendship isn't glued together by fun or usefulness, it's glued together by love (aww!).

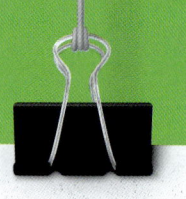

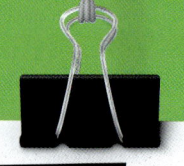

FRIENDS AND ENEMIES

The English word 'friend' comes from the Old English word *freond*. But be careful – don't get it confused with another Old English word, *feond*, which means 'enemy' (we get our modern word 'fiend' from *feond*).

I wonder if we can learn something from this. It doesn't take much to change the word for friend into the word for enemy. There is an idea in the writings of a German philosopher named **Friedrich Nietzsche** that some friendships are destined to end as enemies. Maybe the same things that make us love someone so much can also lead us – if the circumstances go horribly wrong – to hate them?

It definitely happens a lot in books and movies! Take a look at these best friends who turned on each other and became archenemies:

- **Darth Vader and Obi-Wan Kenobi** in *Star Wars*
- **Magneto and Professor X** in *X-Men*
- **Dumbledore and Grindelwald** in *Harry Potter*
- **The Doctor and The Master** in *Doctor Who*

Can you think of other examples?

RESEARCH UPDATE

NEW MESSAGE	
TO: DR MATT @ SHORT & CURLY HQ	
FROM: AGENT ARJUN @ BRAINS TRUST	
SUBJECT: RESEARCH UPDATE ON ZOLA REEVE AND LOUIS FREEMAN	

After recess, Zola tried to sit next to Louis in class, but her friends pulled her away to sit with them instead.

At lunch Zola asked her friends for advice on what to do about Louis. She explained to them what Van said and why she didn't want to invite Louis, even though she did want to try to make friends with him. She asked them for their honest opinions.

Most of Zola's friends agreed with her. They nodded along, told her Van was being 'totally unfair' and that it's her birthday party and she can invite whoever she wants.

However, Zola's best friend, Jen, spoke up and said what she thought. 'I think you're being a bit selfish, Zola,' she said. 'We'd all be happy hanging out with Louis for the day. It would be a nice thing to do. If you wanted to make friends with Louis, you'd go over and talk to him, not sit here talking to us about why you don't want to invite him to your party!'

BOOM! GO, JEN! OH YEAH!

Ahem. I mean, in my professional researcher opinion this was an interesting thing for Jen to say.

It might not surprise you to learn that Zola wasn't happy to hear Jen talking to her like this. Zola went bright red and shouted at Jen, 'So you're taking Van's side? I thought you were my best friend! You're meant to support me, no matter what!'

Then she stormed off, which was pretty dramatic. Except as she was walking away she walked through the middle of an Ultimate Frisbee match and got smacked on the head by the frisbee! I hope she doesn't have a bruise for her birthday party tomorrow.

ZOLA SEEMS PRETTY UPSET WITH JEN. SHOULD JEN HAVE TAKEN ZOLA'S SIDE? WHAT'S MORE IMPORTANT IN FRIENDSHIP – BEING ON THE SAME TEAM OR TELLING EACH OTHER WHAT YOU REALLY THINK?

Agent Arjun signing out

INCOMING PHILOSO-MAIL

NEW MESSAGE

TO: AGENT ARJUN @ BRAINS TRUST
FROM: DR MATT @ SHORT & CURLY HQ
SUBJECT: DR MATT PHILOSO-MAIL

Oh, poor Zola! While she's nursing her sore noggin, I think it would be good if Zola had a think about what she really values in her friends. Does she want them to be utility friends, who just do whatever makes her happy, or does she want true friends who care about whether or not she's a good person?

I think Jen was trying to be a true friend. Remember, true friends care about the virtue of their friends. They admire their friends because they're good people, not because they're just fun or easy to be around. If Jen admires Zola's goodness, she would try to help Zola *keep* being good, and that might involve telling her some things she doesn't want to hear.

Elizabeth Telfer – remember her from earlier? – would have supported Jen. She thought one of the **duties** we have to our friends is to tell them unpleasant truths (when it's necessary). And this sort of makes sense. Caring about our friends should mean wanting them to be the best person they can be.

Dr Matt signing out

THINKING QUESTIONS

1. Should friends always tell each other the truth?

2. It's good to support your friends, but should you support them if you think they're making a bad decision?

3. Zola did try to sit with Louis in class, but she got pulled away. Is she really being as unfriendly as Jen seems to think?

FUN FACTS: INTERNATIONAL FRIENDSHIP DAY

Did you know there's a day when we're all meant to gather together and celebrate friendship? It's called 'International Friendship Day', and it's an event run by the United Nations (UN), so you know it's a big deal.

It's important to have a day to celebrate friendship because the world faces so many complex problems that drive people apart. War, poverty, violence, discrimination and other horrible things are possible because people can't find ways to respect each other and agree about issues.

The UN think friendship represents the opposite of all the worst things in the world. They believe friendship builds relationships based on care, love and trust and that these things are crucial in creating a better world.

So mark 30 July in your calendar and give all your besties a special cuddle. Maybe try to make a new friend! Or, if you're super popular (like me), maybe you could just celebrate world friendship day *every day* . . .

Because you're all my friends, right? Great! Looking forward to receiving my birthday present next year. HINT: I like comic books.

AGENT DEBRIEF

NEW MESSAGE
TO: DR MATT @ SHORT & CURLY HQ
FROM: AGENT ARJUN @ BRAINS TRUST
SUBJECT: AGENT ARJUN – DEBRIEF FOR HQ

I think Van has the best intentions, but he could do with taking some advice from Elizabeth Telfer! It sounds like he's trying to force Zola and Louis to be friends, but that's not really the way it works. It would be great for Louis to find some friends, but Zola can't just flick a switch and become friends with him. It takes time and has to happen naturally.

Looking at the bigger picture though, Van and Jen were right to speak honestly with Zola. They were both being 'true friends' and looking out for her instead of telling her what she wanted to hear.

I like Aristotle's three levels of friendship, and I think it's pretty important to know about them. It helps us to know what is fair to expect of our friends, depending on what kind of friend they are. Perhaps if Zola had known about the different kinds of friendships she wouldn't have been so upset with Jen – she would have understood that Jen had her best interests at heart. And maybe if she'd been more open to inviting 'pleasure friends' as well as her 'best friends' to her party, she might have invited Louis so they could all have fun together.

All this talk of parties has got me thinking about my own birthday, which is in a few weeks. I think we need to get started on the party plans as soon as possible – you can be in charge of the ice cream!

Agent Arjun signing out

BRAVERY

HOLY JALAPEÑO, THAT'S HOT!

MARIO DE LUCA

FIELD RESEARCH REPORT:

SUBJECT: Mario de Luca

DETAILS: Daredevil. Loves to take risks and try new things.

NOTES:

- Should we be allowed to try things even if they're risky or dangerous?
- Why do we get sucked into peer pressure?
- What does it mean to be brave?

AGENT RABIA

REPORT RUN-DOWN

NEW MESSAGE

TO: DR MATT @ SHORT & CURLY HQ
FROM: AGENT RABIA @ BRAINS TRUST
SUBJECT: REPORT RUN-DOWN ON MARIO DE LUCA

There's never a dull moment on a school camp, is there? Mario de Luca and his classmates have headed off on their annual trip, where they'll get to bunk together in caravans, battle the high ropes courses and, after all that, they'll enjoy some of the wonderful food cooked by the cafeteria team at Adventure Valley Conference Centre.

Mario is most excited about the high ropes. He's a total adventure junkie and loves to take risks. He's been climbing trees since he was two – and has a few scars to show for it. He likes to challenge himself, but he also likes the way his classmates look up to him. Whenever there's a pool party, they all want him to do backflips or find something high to jump off into the pool.

On the bus ride to camp there was lots of talk about what Mario's next challenge would be – Mario loved the attention! As the bus pulled into the camp car park, a kid at the back of the bus yelled, 'Hey, Mario! I've got a challenge for you . . . Look at those chillies in the camp garden over there. They look pretty hot. Haha! I challenge you to EAT THEM.'

Everyone on the bus is 100 per cent behind this idea. Everyone except Mario, that is. Mario *HATES* spicy food. He can barely handle pepper, let alone a chilli! Even though he usually loves dares, I don't know if he'll be up for this.

I swear I saw some beads of sweat drip from his nose (imagine what'll happen when he eats the chilli).

As they all piled off the bus, I took the opportunity to do a little research and had a snoop around the Adventure Valley garden. It turns out the cafeteria team here grow all their own fruit and vegetables. These chillies are spectacular! But they are also spectacularly HOT – I think they're jalapeño peppers, which are one of the spiciest chillies around. You know what? I don't blame Mario for being nervous.

So, the whole class wants to see Mario eat a chilli. Well, actually, they want to see him eat a whole peanut butter and chilli sandwich – yuck!

Grossness and spiciness aside, Mario has accepted the dare. He wants everyone to know he's not a chicken. Also, he doesn't want to admit he doesn't like spice because he wants to keep up his reputation as a tough guy.

Personally, I don't think he's thought it through. If he's no good with spice, he's going to look ridiculous after eating a chilli! He'll look like one of those cartoon characters with steam shooting out of his ears. He'll go all red and sweaty and then he'll probably cry. Not the best look for tough guy Mario.

Anyway, earlier today, Mario was scheduled to have his disgusting sandwich of doom. But he got lucky. One of the teachers heard about the challenge and confiscated the sandwich before he could have a bite. Everyone is now banned from going into the garden. Good news for Mario, right?

WRONG. Mario was furious. He spent the next hour arguing with the teacher that he should have the right to decide what he does and doesn't eat. He said, 'Teachers shouldn't be able to make choices about what I do with my body. That's totally unfair – I should be able to eat whatever I want!'

GIVEN MARIO DIDN'T WANT TO EAT THE CHILLI SANDWICH TO BEGIN WITH, I DON'T REALLY GET WHY HE'S SO ANGRY. WHAT'S UP WITH THAT? AND WHY DID MARIO EVEN AGREE IF HE DOESN'T LIKE SPICE? ALSO, DOES HE HAVE A POINT? IS IT EVER OK FOR PEOPLE TO STOP US FROM DOING THINGS THAT ONLY AFFECT US AND OUR OWN BODIES?

Agent Rabia signing out

INCOMING PHILOSO-MAIL

NEW MESSAGE

TO: AGENT RABIA @ BRAINS TRUST
FROM: DR MATT @ SHORT & CURLY HQ
SUBJECT: DR MATT PHILOSO-MAIL

It seems bizarre that anybody would volunteer to eat something they knew they would hate, doesn't it? But I guess there are loads of weird things people do. Think about bungee jumping, skydiving or hot yoga. From the outside, these all seem pretty 'out there' yet many people find these activities fun and meaningful, even if they can also be scary or make you feel uncomfortable.

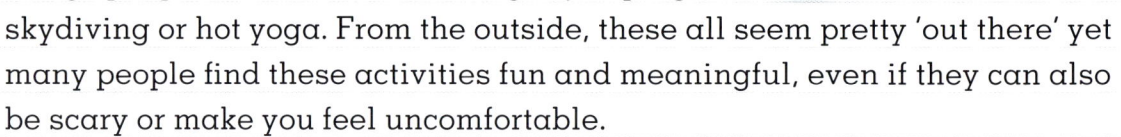

Pain and discomfort aren't necessarily *bad*, and just because an activity isn't all puppy dogs and ice cream doesn't mean it's wrong for people to try it. If Mario is determined to eat a chilli and peanut butter sandwich because he wants to challenge himself, most people would probably say he'd be fine to do so.

If he was an adult, that is.

It's a bit different when it comes to children. That's because we think **consent** – basically your ability to give your permission for something to happen to you – is only possible when you're informed about what might happen. You must be **free** to make the choice for yourself and capable of understanding what might happen. If you have the capacity and the knowledge to make a decision about what's going to happen to you, then you have the **right** to consent to what's happening.

Unfortunately for Mario, most adults tend to assume only adults are wise and mature enough to make these decisions. That's why guardians and parents usually have the right to make medical decisions for their children, and why Mario's teacher decided to step in to stop him from eating the chilli.

These kinds of ideas can be unfair on young people. It assumes they're not very good at making decisions simply because they're young.

That might be true sometimes – after all, experience does help when you're facing a tough question. However, children are often perfectly capable of making decisions for themselves (as I'm sure you know, oh wise and responsible, Rabia).

So, it sounds like Mario's teacher might have needed a **compass to check their assumptions**. Did Mario really need someone else's help to make the right decision? After all, he knew it was going to suck to eat the chilli, but he wanted to do it anyway. It might have been silly, even risky, but he did seem to be able to understand what was going on.

Or did he? After all, some people have died after eating chillies – it's rare, but it happens.

Your detailed field report highlighted an interesting factor, which might suggest Mario wasn't totally able to make the decision for himself. It seems like he was being influenced by **peer pressure**. Mario was so worried about what his friends thought of him, he wasn't really making up his own mind, he was letting other people put pressure on him. When other people try to force us to make a certain decision, that's called **coercion**. Most kinds of coercion are pretty full on – like someone threatening to hurt you if you don't do what they want. We should consider whether Mario's choice is being influenced by the threat of being picked on, mocked or judged by his classmates. If it is, is he making a free choice?

Maybe Mario wasn't free in wanting to eat the sandwich, but are we ever really free? Lots of the things we do – even as adults – are done because we want to fit in or please other people. And because of this, sometimes we do things without truly understanding the consequences. But does that mean we shouldn't be allowed to make these choices?

Dr Matt signing out

THINKING QUESTIONS

1. When do you think someone should be able to make their own decisions, even risky ones, without anybody else interfering?

2. Have you ever done something silly or out of character to try to fit in? Did it work? How did you feel about it?

FUN FACTS:

THE SCOVILLE SCALE OF MOUTH-BURNINESS

Did you know there's an actual scientific scale to measure how hot a chilli is?

It's called the Scoville scale, and it's named after the fella who designed it, an American pharmacist named Wilbur Scoville.

The Scoville scale ranks the spiciness of different chillies based on how much heat-producing chemicals the chilli contains. In the old days, they did this by using volunteer tasters (imagine that job!), but they've got fancier methods now.

Some of the hottest chillies score over a million on the Scoville scale. As a comparison, the jalapeño Mario was going to eat scores about 10,000. So there are chillies more than one hundred times hotter than that!

They've also got really cool names, like 'Carolina Reaper', 'Pepper X', 'The Ghost Chilli' and my favourite 'Dragon's Breath'.

I wouldn't put any of them in a sandwich though.

RESEARCH UPDATE

NEW MESSAGE

TO: DR MATT @ SHORT & CURLY HQ
FROM: AGENT RABIA @ BRAINS TRUST
SUBJECT: RESEARCH UPDATE ON MARIO DE LUCA

I was hoping when the chilli sandwich got confiscated, this was all going to be over – case closed. I had planned to head back to HQ and catch up on some nature documentaries. But I can't – this whole chilli saga has fired up again! (Couldn't resist, sorry! Don't tell Mae I'm making jokes. She won't be happy.)

Let me get you up to speed. Just before everyone went to bed, a couple of people in Mario's class started poking fun at him. They said he was happy the teacher took away the chilli, and that if he was really as brave as he claims, he would sneak into the garden, steal some chillies, come back and eat them. Not long after, the teachers turned out the lights.

Now everyone is lying in bed, wondering what Mario is going to do. And Mario's wondering what he should do. He doesn't want to eat the chillies or get in trouble for sneaking out at night, but he doesn't want to be a chicken either.

I can't help but think about one of my favourite movies, *The Lion King*. The super-wise lion, Mufasa, tells his son, Simba, that being brave doesn't mean you go looking for trouble. I wonder if Mario's seen it. If not, that would be a better way to spend his night, rather than hunting chillies in the dark!

WHAT IS THE BRAVE THING TO DO? SHOULD MARIO PROVE HIS TOUGHNESS BY BREAKING THE RULES AND CHOMPING DOWN ON SOME CHILLIES? IS IT REALLY BRAVE TO DO WHAT EVERYONE ELSE IS TELLING YOU TO DO?

Agent Rabia signing out

INCOMING PHILOSO-MAIL

NEW MESSAGE

TO: AGENT RABIA @ BRAINS TRUST

FROM: DR MATT @ SHORT & CURLY HQ

SUBJECT: DR MATT PHILOSO-MAIL

Sweet *Lion King* reference, Rabia! Not only is it one of my favourite movies (I still know all the words to 'Hakuna Matata'), it's a good example of how we should start thinking about Mario's choice here: by **defining our terms**. What is bravery?

Bravery goes by a few names. It's also called **courage**, and the *really* old-school philosophers used to call it **fortitude**. It's basically about being able to keep doing the right thing even when it's hard, risky or dangerous.

Aristotle, who is probably the biggest name in the courage club (a club I'm definitely keen to be a member of and which I absolutely did not make up), said being courageous was somewhere in between **cowardice** and **recklessness**. Cowardice is when you listen to fear too much, while recklessness is when you don't listen to fear enough. So courage is when we listen to our fears but don't let them control us.

If courage is when we overcome our fear so we can do the right thing, what does this mean? This means that for Mario to be acting bravely, he has to get control over his fear in order to do what's right. Is breaking the

150

rules and giving in to peer pressure doing the right thing? I'm not so sure.

Sometimes bravery isn't just facing fears about getting hurt or injured, it's more to do with overcoming different kinds of fears. It could be about standing up for yourself even if you get made fun of, or doing the right thing even though you might get punished or bullied for it. That's what we call **moral courage**. Tonight, Mario has a great opportunity to practise moral courage.

It seems like what Mario is most afraid of is that other people will think he's not tough anymore. If courage is about not letting fear control us, then the brave thing for Mario to do would be to stand up to the other students, tell them to leave him alone and say he doesn't want to eat the chilli.

This won't be easy for Mario (although it's probably not as hard as eating a Carolina Reaper!). It's also a bit unfair for Mario to be forced into this position. He's not the only one who should be acting bravely!

The students telling him to go steal the chilli aren't being brave either. They're too scared to break the rules themselves – or too scared to eat the chilli – and so are trying to make Mario do it instead.

Are those really the kinds of people Mario should be worried about impressing?

Dr Matt signing out

THINKING QUESTIONS

1. What is the bravest thing you've ever done? What made it brave?

2. Can you be brave when you're doing the wrong thing? Try to think of some examples.

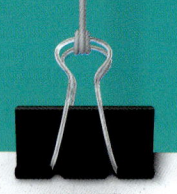

ROBERT KEY – THE BRAVE BOMBARDIER

History is full of great examples of bravery, cowardice and recklessness. Sometimes they are all mixed up in the same story – like the story of British bombardier **Robert Key**.

During World War II, Robert Key was stationed in the French town of Annezin, where part of his job was to keep the people who lived there safe. Sadly, in 1944 he died in the town after being injured in a hand grenade accident.

For over 60 years, the official record said he had been killed because he was 'showing off' with a hand grenade. I'm not sure what showing off with a grenade actually looks like. Maybe he was trying to juggle with it? Or he was trying to balance it on his nose like a seal? Who knows!

Anyway, his fooling around was reckless. He should have been more careful with the hand grenade, but unfortunately his recklessness got him good.

Or did it? Here's a twist for you. Recently, some French historians were doing some research into what happened in the town during the war and they uncovered a totally different story about how Robert Key died.

During a patrol through Annezin, Robert saw a group of children gathered around a live hand grenade. He quickly saw the danger they were in, snatched the grenade and ran as far away from the group of kids as he could before the grenade – and poor old Bob – blew up.

It turns out Robert, who was for a long time remembered as being a reckless knucklehead who met an unfortunate end, was a hero.

AGENT DEBRIEF

NEW MESSAGE

TO: DR MATT @ SHORT & CURLY HQ
FROM: AGENT RABIA @ BRAINS TRUST
SUBJECT: AGENT RABIA – DEBRIEF FOR HQ

This is a really tricky case. I found it hard to understand why Mario would do something he was clearly going to hate, but when I think about how his friends were pressuring him, it kind of makes sense. What's worse: disappointing your friends or eating a spicy chilli?

Mario's teacher also made a big assumption: that Mario was too young to know what he was doing. But I wonder if that's true – and even if it is, does it matter? Adults make dumb decisions all the time and usually nobody is allowed to stop them. Why is it so different for kids?

Agent Rabia signing out

FIGHTING

PYJAMMY WHAMMY!

DEV NAYAR

FIELD RESEARCH REPORT:

SUBJECT: Dev Nayar

DETAILS: Wore his jammies to school and fought back against his bullies.

NOTES:

- What's the difference between joking and teasing?
- Can you fight back against a bully?
- Do we need to stick up for our friends if it means we might get hurt?

AGENT ARJUN

REPORT RUN-DOWN

NEW MESSAGE
TO: DR MATT @ SHORT & CURLY HQ
FROM: AGENT ARJUN @ BRAINS TRUST
SUBJECT: REPORT RUN-DOWN ON DEV NAYAR

We've just got word that a student at a nearby school has shown up in his pyjamas! THIS IS NOT A DRILL – there is a boy in class wearing his jammies. I know, hilarious. I wonder if he's got slippers on too. That would be so good.

I mean. Ahem, back to the serious field research report . . .

Research subject Dev Nayar showed up at school in his pyjamas today. Dev's school is holding a 'pyjama day' fundraiser for the school soccer team. Unfortunately for Dev, his mum got the dates mixed up. The fundraiser is actually next week, but his mum thought it was today – whoops! Dev is really embarrassed – everyone is laughing at him.

During class Dev's best friend, Kara, passed him a note that said, 'Are you sleepy? Do you need a nap?' Dev smiled and wrote back, 'Not yet, but I'll probably need one after talking to you all recess. You're so BORING!'

At recess, while Dev and Kara were hanging out, some other kids who have been picking on Dev since Year One, started making jokes. They called him 'Dozey Dev' and asked if he wanted a bottle of milk. Then a whole bunch of them started singing lullabies to him.

Once they went away, Kara went to sit with him. He was pretty mad at her, which was a bit funny to watch because he was still in his jammies. He said,

'If you're my friend, you should stick up for me when I'm being bullied. You could have at least gone to get a teacher.'

Kara was confused. Dev thought it was funny when *she* had made a joke, so why did he care when other people did it?

Besides, Kara thought, if she'd stood up for him they might have started picking on her instead. Also, if she'd gone to a teacher, everyone would have picked on her. Nobody likes a dobber. (Side note: is this true? Is it sometimes OK to dob? Sorry, that's a totally different question.)

> I'M SO CONFUSED. WAS KARA A BAD FRIEND? WAS IT WRONG FOR HER TO PROTECT HERSELF? DID SHE DO THE WRONG THING?

Agent Arjun signing out

INCOMING PHILOSO-MAIL

NEW MESSAGE

TO: AGENT ARJUN @ BRAINS TRUST
FROM: DR MATT @ SHORT & CURLY HQ
SUBJECT: DR MATT PHILOSO-MAIL

Hey, Arjun! I can understand why you're confused – that's a tricky one. But before you get a headache, let's see if we can get to the bottom of this. First, we need to figure out why Dev thought Kara's note was OK but didn't like the way the other kids treated him at recess. Looks like Dev made an important **distinction** today – and that's exactly what we're going to do.

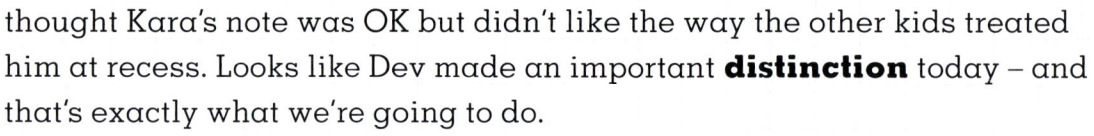

The **distinction** is between **joking** and **bullying**. Sometimes they can look the same, but there are important details that make them VERY different. Bullying is when you use your power over somebody to make them feel bad about themselves. It usually happens over a period of time. Jokes, on the other hand, are more of a one-time thing. It sounds like when Kara teased her mate Dev, he knew she was joking, so the things she said didn't make him feel bad. But the other kids did.

Those kids might say they were just having fun with Dev too. They might have even said, 'Hey, man, it was just a joke!' But because they've been making fun of him for years, it's more likely they were being bullies. Even if they weren't, there's still a problem with what they did because they weren't paying attention to how it was making Dev feel.

Bullying and teasing can sometimes happen by accident. This is why it's so important to get out our **torches** and use **empathy and curiosity** to try to imagine and understand how other people might be feeling. If the other kids had done that, they might have understood why it was cool for Kara to joke with Dev but not OK for them to do the same thing.

I should point out, our imagination is never perfect – you might have the most vivid imagination EVER, but you'll never know what your pet goldfish is thinking. You're just too different!

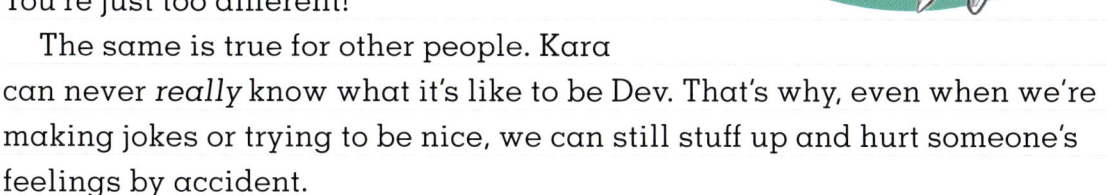

The same is true for other people. Kara can never *really* know what it's like to be Dev. That's why, even when we're making jokes or trying to be nice, we can still stuff up and hurt someone's feelings by accident.

Even though we can't always rely on the power of our imagination to understand *exactly* what others might be feeling, it's still pretty good and it's the best tool we've got to **empathise** in tricky situations. So we need to give it a workout every now and then. The kids who picked on Dev definitely should have used their imaginations . . .

But it's not just the bullies who needed to use their imagination – Kara did too! If she'd imagined herself in Dev's shoes, she probably could have figured out that he needed help during recess. This is why our imagination is important – it's like an ethical superpower that helps us work out what other people need without them having to ask. One version of this is what philosophers call **The Golden Rule** – TREAT OTHER PEOPLE THE WAY WE WOULD LIKE TO BE TREATED.

Once Kara figures out that Dev might like some help, then it gets CURLIER. What if helping Dev means turning herself into a target?

Most of the time, ethics helps us work out the right thing to do, but it doesn't always tell us the safest or easiest thing to do. It would definitely be safer for Kara not to say anything, and it is very important that we take care of ourselves, but think about it this way: what would Kara want Dev to do if he saw her being bullied? Would she want him to stay quiet and protect himself or try to help her out?

Dr Matt signing out

THINKING QUESTIONS

1. Put yourself in Dev's shoes – or slippers, in this case! You're the only person at school in your PJs. How would you feel?

2. Do you think there is a difference between jokes, teasing and bullying?

3. Imagine your friend is being bullied. You can stand up for your friend, but then the bullies will turn on you! Would it be OK to do nothing?

FUN FACTS

- More than a quarter of kids between Year Four and Year Nine are bullied every few weeks or more.

- More students are now picked on online than in person.

- It's not just a problem for young people – half of all Australians have been bullied at work.

Actually, these facts aren't much fun at all . . .

THE GOLDEN RULE

TREAT OTHER PEOPLE THE WAY YOU WOULD LIKE TO BE TREATED.

This idea has appeared in lots of different philosophical writings throughout history. A major source is the *Bible*, where it says, 'Do unto others as you would have them do unto you'.

Another version comes from a German philosopher named **Immanuel Kant** – you might remember him from his thoughts about promises. His ideas on how we treat others and our promises are pretty similar. He thought we were only allowed to do things that we'd be OK with other people doing in the same situation. If it's acceptable for you to steal a cookie because you're hungry, you'd have to be OK with every person stealing a cookie when they're hungry – even if they steal it from you! Kant didn't think we could ever make a special exception for ourselves.

RESEARCH UPDATE

NEW MESSAGE

TO: DR MATT @ SHORT & CURLY HQ
FROM: AGENT ARJUN @ BRAINS TRUST
SUBJECT: RESEARCH UPDATE ON DEV NAYAR

Ohh boy, Dev is in **SO MUCH TROUBLE!** At lunch the kids came back and started bullying him again — pulling on his pyjamas and trying to 'tuck him into bed' — and he snapped! He grabbed a stick and started hitting one of the kids on the arm with it. (He's actually got a pretty good swing. I wonder if he plays tennis. That's probably not relevant.) What is relevant is that the stick bounced off the kid's arm and hit him in the face, and now he's got a bleeding nose! That part was an accident. Still, maybe Dev went too far.

Now Dev's going to the principal's office and will probably get a serious telling-off, but isn't that unfair? The bullies started it. They were grabbing him and pushing him around.

DOESN'T DEV HAVE THE RIGHT TO FIGHT BACK? I KNOW VIOLENCE IS BAD, BUT SOMETIMES WE HAVE TO DEFEND OURSELVES, RIGHT?

Agent Arjun signing out

INCOMING PHILOSO-MAIL

NEW MESSAGE

TO: AGENT ARJUN @ BRAINS TRUST
FROM: DR MATT @ SHORT & CURLY HQ
SUBJECT: DR MATT PHILOSO-MAIL

Sometimes we do have to defend ourselves, and it's totally OK to do so. Violence is usually bad and shouldn't be your go-to solution, but – and this is a BIG BUT (with only one 'T' – a BIG BUTT with two 'Ts' is something very different) – if it's the only way to protect ourselves against a baddie, most people (and philosophers) would say it's OK in order to keep safe.

However, and listen up because this part is important, you can't use more violence than you need. Did Dev really need to bash his bully with a stick? Or could he have just pushed the bully to protect himself?

Some people might say, 'Stuff pushing, the stick worked. Next time that bully will think twice before messing with Dev!' These people think we should do whatever works and forget about the rules. Is this the best approach?

Let's take that thought into our ideas lab and do a **thought experiment**.

Imagine someone is flicking you in the ear. It's really annoying, they shouldn't be doing it and you want them to stop. You could slap away their hand, but that would only stop them for a bit. They might start flicking you again later. So instead, you decide to pull out a GIANT SAMURAI SWORD and chop off their hand. Now they can NEVER flick your ear again!

Which response is the right one?

If you said the slap was a better response than the samurai sword, that's because you think something called **proportionality** matters. Proportionality is a fancy word philosophers and lawyers use. It means balancing the way we treat people against the way they treat us. If someone picks on you a little bit, it would be wrong for you to be *really* mean in return. The samurai sword response is bad because it is **disproportionate**. It does more damage to them than they were doing to you.

Even when it's ethically OK to protect ourselves, we have to make sure we're only using the amount of violence necessary to keep us safe, and make sure we're not doing more harm to the bully than the bully is doing to us.

It's hard to figure out this stuff in the heat of the moment. When you're scared, angry or worked up, it's difficult to take the time to think things through. It's almost impossible when people are pushing and shoving you! So even if Dev did more than was necessary, we shouldn't be too harsh on him. After all, he was put into a stressful situation by the bullies and that wasn't his fault.

But remember, it's always important to get out those **hiking poles** and **question our emotions** rather than follow them blindly. They're not always a good guide to what's right.

Dr Matt signing out

THINKING QUESTIONS

1. Why do you think some people bully others?

2. Have you ever fought back against a bully? Did it work?

3. What are some non-violent ways of stopping someone from picking on you?

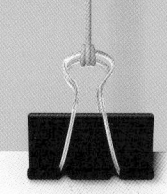

CASEY HEYNES

In 2011, a video appeared online where a small, skinny boy was punching, teasing and bullying a taller boy. The small boy's name is Richard. The tall boy's name is Casey.

Richard punches Casey a few times and pushes him against a wall. Other students are laughing at Casey and filming it on their phones. Then, it all changes. Casey grabs Richard, flips him up in the air and slams him facedown into the cement. Richard gets up looking very hurt and really shaky.

The video went viral. It turned out Casey had been bullied a lot at school and finally decided to stand up for himself. He was celebrated for his anti-bullying stance and was even brought on stage at a Justin Bieber concert!

But it turns out Richard – the bully – had also been bullied most of his life. Richard also said Casey had started the fight by teasing him in the corridors at school. The video only shows the fight, but we don't know what happened beforehand.

Sometimes the world doesn't split nicely into bullies and victims. Lots of bullies have also been picked on in their own lives. They learn to attack first, before someone attacks them. That's not the right thing to do, but in a way, they're just trying to protect themselves too.

A PHILOSOPHER'S GUIDE TO FIGHTING BACK

1. Do you need to fight back? Is there another way of ending the fight and protecting yourself?

2. Only use as much violence as is necessary to stop the bullying.

3. Don't do more harm to the bully than they have been doing to you.

4. Violence can protect you in the short term, but it's not usually a long-term solution! A philosopher named **Hannah Arendt** once said that, 'violence is like a language that only understands itself'. If you speak violence to someone, they'll speak it back to you. So if you actually want to stop the fighting for good, you'll need to try something different. Go and seek advice from an authority figure – like a teacher or parent – they might have some ideas or strategies you hadn't thought of.

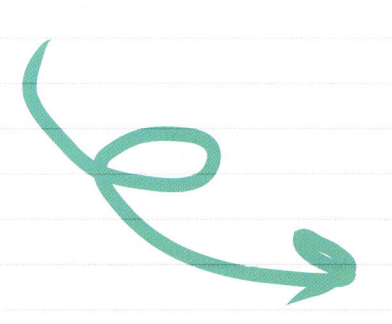

> **REMEMBER:**
> THIS IS HARD TO DO IN THE HEAT OF THE MOMENT, BUT THE MORE WE PRACTICE, THE EASIER IT GETS.

AGENT DEBRIEF

NEW MESSAGE
TO: DR MATT @ SHORT & CURLY HQ
FROM: AGENT ARJUN @ BRAINS TRUST
SUBJECT: AGENT ARJUN – DEBRIEF FOR HQ

When I started observing Dev's pyjama fiasco, I thought it'd be really funny. But that meant I probably didn't pay enough attention to the fact that Dev was very embarrassed. I guess that's why **curiosity and empathy** are so important, right?

Things got seriously curly when Dev decided to fight back – even though Dev was the victim, he couldn't just do whatever he wanted to protect himself. The bully was totally in the wrong, but there are still rules like necessity and proportionality that apply to Dev.

Looking at the bigger picture, these ideas seem pretty similar to the way we think about soldiers fighting wars, the way police can treat criminals and how those criminals are punished when the police catch them. They can be applied to sport as well – if your opponent is cheating, it doesn't mean you should do the same thing. To be a good sport you have to win fairly.

So I guess, even when you're fighting a bully, maybe you have to fight fairly. But does that make it easier for the bullies to keep picking on Dev? And isn't that unfair? Oh boy, I need a nap. Is it pyjama day at HQ?

Agent Arjun signing out

INTEGRITY

INTEGRITY

MORAL COMPASS

DISHONESTY

FUDGING FRENCH

AIKA SATO

FIELD RESEARCH REPORT:

SUBJECT: Aika Sato

DETAILS: Wants to get good marks on her next exam so she can go to a theme park during the holidays.

NOTES:

- Is it OK to do the wrong thing if nobody's looking?
- How do we resist temptations to do the wrong thing?
- Do we have to own up if we make a mistake?

AGENT MAE

REPORT RUN-DOWN

NEW MESSAGE

TO: DR MATT @ SHORT & CURLY HQ
FROM: AGENT MAE @ BRAINS TRUST
SUBJECT: REPORT RUN-DOWN ON AIKA SATO

Aika Sato has been studying harder than ever before. Her parents think she could do better at school, so they've made her a deal. If she gets more than 90 per cent on her next exam, she can go to any amusement park she wants during the holidays. There are a few near Aika's house she could choose from, so it's hard to decide. Does she go to Action Zone, the one with the fastest roller-coaster in the country? Or Watertopia, the one where you get to swim with dolphins?

Unless Aika gets good marks, it won't matter – she won't get to go.

And to make things worse, her next exam is French, which Aika finds really hard. She's been trying to learn all the words and is starting to get the hang of the different verbs, but she's still struggling with past, present and future tenses.

I don't blame her. That stuff looks complicated. I only know one word in French – *oeuf*, it means 'egg'. The reason I know that word is because it lets me tell the best joke ever!

Why do you only eat one egg for breakfast in France? Because in France, one egg is an oeuf!

Get it? Because 'an *oeuf*' sounds like 'enough'. Classic comedy.

Anyway, French is hard. Aika is worried she won't get a high enough mark. But something happened to Aika at school that might change everything.

I had been observing Aika all day – being super-stealthy so no one would notice me – and followed her to her PE class. I found an ideal spot to keep watch and take notes behind a tree. Aika is an awesome netball player – this girl's got skills, but as she was about to shoot for the goal she tripped and her shoelace broke. She tried to keep playing, but her shoe kept coming off. It nearly hit someone in the head! So Aika decided to go back to the classroom early to get changed.

Her French teacher, Madame Dubois, was already setting up for their next class. As Aika walked into the classroom, Madame Dubois realised she had left something in the staff room. '*Sacre bleu!*' she yelled, and walked out the door, leaving Aika alone in the classroom.

Aika's shoelace was still broken, so she started looking around for some string to use as a temporary fix. Here's where it got *curly*. Madame Dubois had left some papers on her desk, including – you guessed it – next week's French exam! As Aika was nosing around for string, she spotted the exam and her eyes nearly popped out of her head!

This is Aika's moment. She could pinch a copy of the test, write down the questions and memorise the answers. She'd get full marks and it'd be theme park city this holidays!

WE'RE USUALLY TOLD CHEATING IS WRONG, BUT AIKA HAS BEEN STUDYING REALLY HARD. WOULD IT BE SO BAD FOR HER TO TAKE THE TEST JUST THIS ONCE? SHE WOULDN'T GET CAUGHT – NOBODY WOULD KNOW!

Agent Mae signing out

INCOMING PHILOSO-MAIL

NEW MESSAGE

TO: AGENT MAE @ BRAINS TRUST
FROM: DR MATT @ SHORT & CURLY HQ
SUBJECT: DR MATT PHILOSO-MAIL

Ne touchez pas à cet examen, Aika!

Nice job, Mae – this situation is curly indeed, but not for the usual reasons.

Some of the curly situations we find ourselves in are hard because we don't know what is the right thing to do. Other times what's hard is that we know what we should do, but it's difficult to follow through and do it. Philosophers have fancy names for each of these. The first ones are called **ethical dilemmas** and the second ones are called **moral temptations**. We should use our **machetes** to **spot the difference** between them.

When we're facing an ethical dilemma, there's not always one right or wrong thing to do. All the options have something good or something bad about them. When we're facing a moral temptation, there is an obviously right thing to do, but there are costs to doing the right thing, and we're tempted to do the wrong thing because we don't want to pay the costs.

Aika is definitely facing a moral temptation between a good thing and a bad thing. She wants to do the wrong thing – she wants to cheat so she can go to a theme park (and let's be clear: both theme parks sound awesome!).

This is a moral temptation because Aika is only thinking about doing it because she won't get caught. In cases like this, it's useful to use **The Sunlight Test**. This idea has been around for a while, but it's usually credited to an American judge named **Louis Brandeis**, who said, 'sunlight is the best disinfectant and light is the best policeman'.

What he meant was, it's easy to do the wrong thing in the dark when nobody knows. But if we imagined that *everyone* was going to find out what we did, then we might be less likely to do the wrong thing.

Imagine if Aika cheated and it wound up on the front page of the school newsletter. Tomorrow, the headline might say, *AIKA SATO: BIG STINKY CHEATER* (she's stinky because she's just done PE). Now, let's imagine if she didn't cheat – what would the headline say? *AIKA SATO: VERY HONEST PERSON*. Which headline would Aika prefer?

The Sunlight Test – basically, only do it if you'd be OK with the consequences of being caught – is a test of **integrity**. It asks us to walk the talk and be who we say we are, no matter who is watching.

One last thought about moral temptations. When we reward people for their achievements, it can encourage people to do sneaky things (not good sneaky like you, Mae – bad sneaky) to get the job done and collect their reward. The reward *is* a temptation to do the wrong thing!

It makes me wonder, if Aika's parents had said she could go to a theme park if she studied hard, no matter what mark she got, would she be less tempted to cheat?

Dr Matt signing out

THINKING QUESTIONS

1. Is it OK to break the rules sometimes?

2. If Aika cheats, is it her fault? Or is it her parents' fault for creating the temptation? Or maybe her teacher's for leaving the exam on her desk?

HISTORY'S FAMOUS CHEATERS

Even the best of us can be tempted to do the wrong thing sometimes. Here are some people who are considered heroes by many, but who have also been found guilty of cheating at some point in time.

Lance Armstrong

The superman of cycling, Lance Armstrong, was everyone's inspiration story. He won the Tour de France, road cycling's most difficult race, a record seven times in a row, and after battling cancer!

Throughout Armstrong's career, lots of questions and rumours had circulated about whether he had been using performance-enhancing drugs – there were suggestions they were really common in cycling. In 2013, after denying it for years, he finally admitted to using drugs. He said he didn't feel bad about cheating because everyone was doing it.

Even though lots of people still respect him, it was an eye-opening moment when somebody who was everyone's hero quickly turned into the villain.

Jane Goodall

This lady is awesome. She's become extremely famous for her work with chimpanzees, but is also a devoted animal-rights activist and environmentalist. Unfortunately, she's also been guilty of being a copycat – in academic terms, **a plagiarist**.

Plagiarism is when you copy someone else's work and pretend it's your own. In 2013, Goodall was going to publish a book called *Seeds of Hope*, but a few reviewers noticed some of the book had been copied and pasted from websites like Wikipedia! Goodall issued an apology and said it was because she'd put the book together quickly, meaning she'd forgotten to rewrite or edit certain sections.

Diego Maradona

Maybe the most well-known act of cheating in history happened in the 1986 Football World Cup quarter-final, where Argentina were playing England. Argentinian superstar Diego Maradona was at the peak of his career.

During the match, Maradona scored two of football's most memorable goals. One was an amazing piece of skill, where he dribbled past five England players to score. The other is remembered for all the wrong reasons.

It's called 'The Hand of God'. Here's what happened – after some very clever build-up play, the ball was chipped in front of the England goalkeeper. Maradona jumped out to try to head the ball into the goal, but instead of hitting the ball with his head, he managed to sneak his hand in there and punch the ball over the keeper and into the goal. The ref missed it, and the goal stood.

Argentina went on to win 2-1, meaning it was 'The Hand of God' that made the difference that day. People still talk about it whenever the two teams meet on the football pitch.

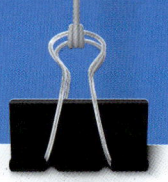

Trevor Chappell

Here's a tricky one – you're going to have to decide for yourself whether this counts as cheating or not! During a cricket match between Australia and New Zealand, the game went down to the final ball. New Zealand needed six runs to win – which is possible in cricket, but only if you hit a HUGE shot that goes over the boundary on the full. To do this, you need to get a lot of power under the ball.

The Australian bowler who needed to bowl the last ball was Trevor Chappell. His brother, Greg, was the captain at the time. He told Trevor to bowl the last ball underarm – basically, roll the ball along the ground – which would stop the batsman from getting under the ball with enough power to hit a six.

Technically, bowling underarm wasn't against the rules, but it was still considered so badly against the spirit of the game that both the Australian and New Zealand Prime Ministers criticised the decision! What do you think? Even though it was within the rules, was this a type of cheating?

RESEARCH UPDATE

NEW MESSAGE

TO: DR MATT @ SHORT & CURLY HQ
FROM: AGENT MAE @ BRAINS TRUST
SUBJECT: RESEARCH UPDATE ON AIKA SATO

It looks like the temptation was too strong for Aika. She swiped the exam while Madame Dubois was *en haut* (upstairs – I've been practising my French while observing Aika). But then things got complicated.

Aika was about to start taking photos of the exam on her phone when she seemed to have second thoughts. She didn't say anything, but she was shaking her head and looking unsure. Then she started to walk back towards the teacher's desk to put the exam back, without peeking. Hooray! Aika had a change of heart!

Except, before she could return it, Madame Dubois walked into the room. Thinking fast, Aika stuffed the exam down the back of her shorts and went to get changed. She decided she'd try to sneak it back onto the desk later. (I could help with that – did you know I'm really sneaky? Of course not. I'M TOO SNEAKY FOR YOU TO NOTICE.)

Unfortunately, today has not been Aika's day. She's been having the WORST luck – it's getting hard to watch! About halfway through the class, Madame Dubois realised the exam was missing. She was *furieux* about it.

Everyone was looking around, wondering who did it, but Aika didn't budge. Madame Dubois continued with the lesson, but said nobody was going to lunch until she found out who was responsible.

Aika just wrote a note to her bestie. I'm gonna sneak in closer and see if I can get a peek. OK, here's what it says.

> You can't tell anybody, but it was me who stole the exam. I didn't even look at it though! I was going to, but I changed my mind. I was just really nervous about not getting a good enough mark to go to the theme park, you know? But I realised it was wrong and I was going to put it back when Dubois came into the room.
>
> What should I do? If I own up now, she'll think I was cheating and I'll get zero for the exam. But I WASN'T going to cheat. I honestly changed my mind, but she'll never believe me! And my parents will be so mad!

WOULD IT BE OK FOR AIKA TO STAY QUIET OR SHOULD SHE OWN UP TO WHAT SHE DID? AFTER ALL, SHE DID EVENTUALLY TRY TO DO THE RIGHT THING. IT WOULD BE WRONG IF PEOPLE THOUGHT SHE WAS A CHEATER, WOULDN'T IT?

Agent Mae signing out

INCOMING PHILOSO-MAIL

NEW MESSAGE

TO: AGENT MAE @ BRAINS TRUST
FROM: DR MATT @ SHORT & CURLY HQ
SUBJECT: DR MATT PHILOSO-MAIL

Oh, Aika – it's quite the pickle she's got herself into. Nothing seems to be going her way!

I don't think Aika has much choice here though. It doesn't sound like Madame Dubois is going to budge. Plus, by staying quiet, Aika is making all her classmates suffer, even though they did nothing wrong.

I should point out before we go on, I'm not convinced Madame Dubois' methods are totally ethical here either. She's punishing innocent people as a way to force the guilty person to own up. That's really unfair.

Imagine if a worker at a company was stealing from the business and the boss announced, 'Unless the thief owns up, I'm going to fire everyone!' We'd think that was very unfair, but is there anything different in what is happening here?

Let's get back to Aika's sticky situation. I understand why she doesn't want to confess. She thinks that, because she didn't *see* the exam, she hasn't actually cheated and doesn't deserve to be punished. Let's use a **thought experiment** to see if this reasoning makes sense.

> Let's imagine you break into a museum and steal some rare art (you know, because you're sneaky). You're about to hop in the van and drive away to sell it on the black market when you change your mind. You realise you're doing the wrong thing and go to put it back on the wall, but the security guards see you. Should they let you go because you changed your mind, or should you be punished because you did steal the artwork?

179

Aika knows she did the wrong thing, she just doesn't want to face the **consequences** of what she's done. That's understandable, especially because she thinks no one will believe she didn't actually cheat. Aika shouldn't get punished for cheating, because she didn't cheat. But she did steal, and it's worth thinking whether she deserves to be punished for that. It would be unfair if Aika was punished more than she deserves, but she can't know for sure what punishment she's going to get until she admits what she did. Ethics is all about **responsibility**. We are only able to be ethical because we can make choices, but part of being able to make choices is the fact we have to accept responsibility for them. We get praised when we do the right thing and we get blamed when we do the wrong thing. It might not be pleasant, but it's part of the deal.

Still, Aika is less likely to admit what she's done if she thinks she's going to be treated unfairly. This is an important point to bear in mind – sometimes the fear of a punishment that's too harsh can make it harder for people to do the right thing, even when they want to.

This is a nice reminder of why we need to use our **torches** to practise **curiosity and empathy** for people who have done the wrong thing when we're breaking down these kinds of issues. It's really easy to point the finger and make judgements, but what's more useful is trying to understand *why* someone did the wrong thing, whether there are any reasons to be more lenient on them, and to remember that we will *all* fail to be the best version of ourselves at one point or another.

How would we like other people to treat us if we got caught doing the wrong thing?

Dr Matt signing out

THINKING QUESTIONS

1. Have you ever had to own up to doing something wrong? How did it go?

2. If you were one of Aika's classmates, what would you want her to do?

3. Is it fair for Madame Dubois to hold the whole class back because one person did the wrong thing?

FUN FACTS: I'M SPARTACUS!

Here's one way Aika could get out of her sticky situation. She could get *everyone* to say they stole the exam. Picture this: Aika stands up and says, 'I stole it'. Then her bestie stands up and says, 'No, I stole it'. Eventually, everyone in the class does the same thing.

That's what happens in one of the most famous moments in movie history: *Spartacus*. Spartacus was a slave in ancient Rome who trained as a gladiator, so he knew how to fight. He used those skills to escape with some fellow slaves and built up a slave army.

In the end, he was defeated and his army was treated pretty horribly. About 6000 of them were crucified on the road back to Rome.

In 1960, a movie based on Spartacus' life came out and added some pretty dramatic elements to the story. In the movie, once the slaves had been defeated, the Romans offer the surviving slaves a deal. They won't be killed, they'll return to their lives as slaves, so long as they identify their leader, Spartacus.

Just as Spartacus is about to hand himself in, one of his friends stands up and says, 'I'm Spartacus!', then someone else claims to be Spartacus. Eventually, the whole army is yelling, 'I'm Spartacus!'

Although there's no reason to think that actually happened, it's a pretty nice example of how a group of people refused to let someone they cared about suffer an unfair punishment alone. They decided they'd all be in it together.

Of course, they then all ended up being crucified, so it doesn't always lead to a happy ending.

AGENT DEBRIEF

NEW MESSAGE
TO: DR MATT @ SHORT & CURLY HQ
FROM: AGENT MAE @ BRAINS TRUST
SUBJECT: AGENT MAE – DEBRIEF FOR HQ

I feel so sorry for Aika. It seems a bit unfair that a single bad decision – one she regrets and wishes she could take back – is going to cost her, big time. If only she'd had better shoelaces, she would never have been tempted by that test.

All of this makes me think about forgiveness. Aika would totally own up to her mistake if she knew people were going to forgive her. Unfortunately, sometimes people take a long time to forgive – or they might hold a grudge forever!

I always thought ethics was about 'goodies' and 'baddies', but Aika's case makes it seem way more complicated than that. She's a good person, but she did the wrong thing. That makes everything so much curlier.

OK, now before I come back, mind if I head over to Paris to test out my new French skills? No? Great. *Au revoir!*

Agent Mae signing out

FINAL PHILOSO-MAIL

NEW MESSAGE	_ ⤢ ✕
TO: SHORT & CURLY READERS	
FROM: DR MATT @ SHORT & CURLY HQ	
SUBJECT: YOUR MISSION	

Well, intrepid ethics-plorer, here we are at the end of the book. This adventure into the world of Short & Curly is over.

OR IS IT?

Like any great explorer, I don't want you to stop just because you've reached the end. This isn't a book designed to be picked up, read and then put aside to collect dust. Every now and then, pick it up and read through one of the research reports. You might find that as you learn new things, have new experiences and continue to ask questions about how the world should be, some of your answers to those questions change.

More importantly, I don't want you to keep your adventures in ethics within the world of Short & Curly. While you read this book, I'm certain you would have thought of examples from your own life where these sticky, tricky ethical questions apply. And that's the point – your whole world is jam-packed with ethical issues.

Which leads me to one final research assignment – FOR YOU!

I want you to keep wondering about why the world is the way it is. Whenever you hear someone say 'that's just the way it is', 'the way we normally do things is like this' or 'everybody knows that's wrong', I want you to open your ethical toolkit and get to work.

Keep challenging ideas about what's 'normal', question whether people's ideas about what's good and bad make sense, and most importantly, keep caring about making the best choices you can, and helping the world be the best it can be.

Oh! And make sure you report back. On the next page there's an email address where you can send any questions, ideas or discoveries to – I'm already sitting at my computer, waiting for them to arrive.

But not for long. The Brains Trust and I have heard some of the elves at Santa's workshop are going on strike. We're off to the North Pole to investigate!

Now, where did I put my gloves . . .

See you next time, Agent.

Dr Matt signing out

THE SHORT & CURLY PODCAST

The *Short & Curly* podcast takes you on super-fun, ridiculous and eye-opening journeys to all kinds of ethical questions, big and small. It's hosted by the awesome duo, Molly Daniels and Carl Smith, and features philosopher Dr Matt Beard from The Ethics Centre, who gives some ethical insight into the weird and wacky dilemmas.

Short & Curly is produced by ABC Audio Studios, and is the brainchild of genius producer Kyla Slaven (who also co-wrote this book).

There are loads of shows to listen to and more coming all the time. Here's a taste of some of the adventures we've gone on so far:

- **Can you eat your pets?**
- **What's wrong with travelling to Mars?**
- **Is it ethical to climb Mt Everest?**
- **Should we let chimpanzees come to school with us?**
- **Can a robot be your best buddy?**
- **Why can't kids vote in elections?**

Listen to these episodes, and so many others, wherever you get your podcasts. If you need help finding the episodes, you can go to our website **www.abc.net.au/radio/programs/shortandcurly**

Aaaand don't forget to send us your big ethical questions, ideas and research findings. You're part of team Short & Curly now – we need your help discovering new dilemmas, stories and curly issues to explore! Email us at **shortandcurly@abc.net.au**

One more thing – don't keep us a secret! Tell your friends, your teachers and your pet foxes to listen to our show as well. There's always room for one more person in the Brains Trust.

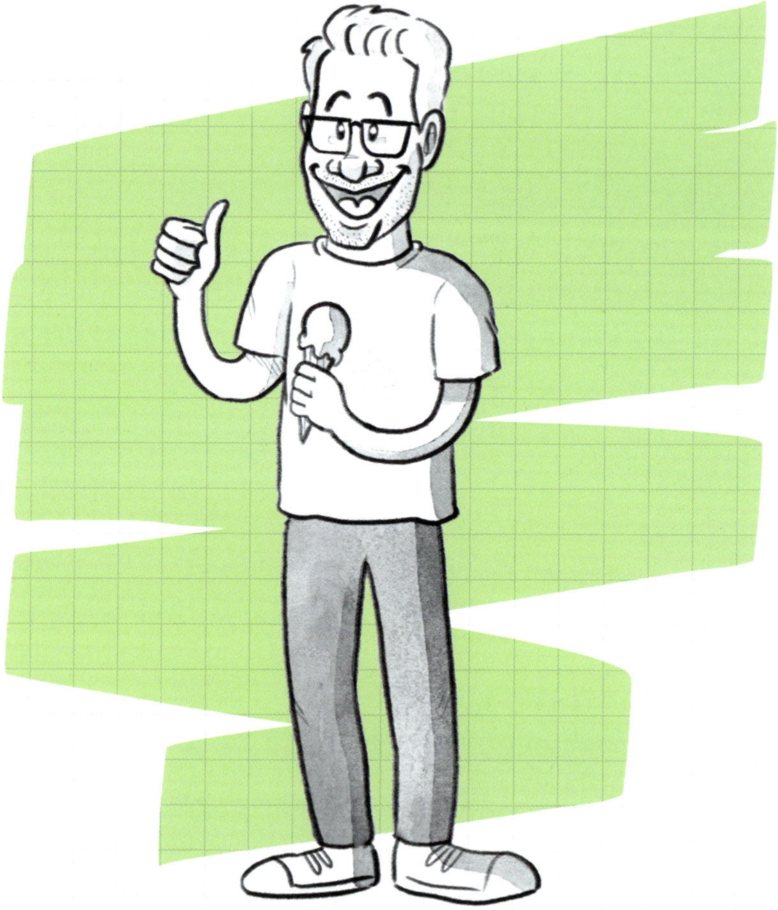

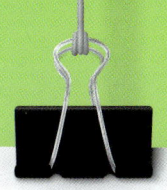

Dr Matt Beard is a husband, dad, pop culture nerd, moral philosopher and ethicist. Matt is a Fellow at The Ethics Centre and the resident philosopher for the kids' ethics podcast *Short & Curly*. He appears regularly in print, on the radio and TV, to discuss ethical issues from vampires to anti-vaccination. Matt believes everyone is already a philosopher who, given the right circumstances and skills, can live a wise, enriched and ethical life.

* * *

I would like to thank the Hollys at Penguin Random House, who understood this project from the start, were excited, supportive and helped bring our ideas to life.

Simon's drawings capture the fun and liveliness of philosophy and ethics when it's done the way it should be. Thanks for making this book beautiful.

The team at The Ethics Centre have let me disappear for random weeks at less than ideal times to record new episodes. Thanks for having my back.

Kyla, Molly and Carl – team Short & Curly – you're ridiculous, hilarious and so patient with my awful jokes. Thanks for bringing a nerdy philosopher along for the ride.

Mum and Dad, you gave me the freedom to question and the respect to accept my answers – even when you disagreed. Thanks for teaching me to think.

Jenn, you're my torch, compass, hiking poles and everything in between. Thanks for helping me be me.

Darwin, here's to every curious conversation we haven't had yet. Thanks for showing me the wonder in the world.

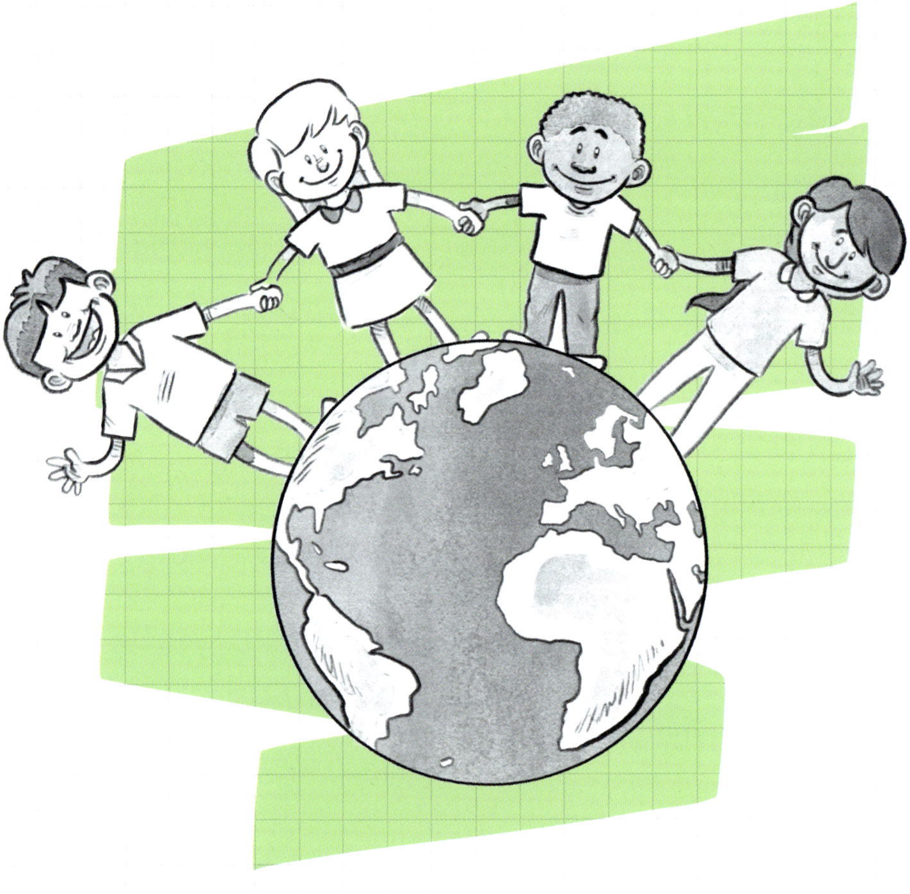

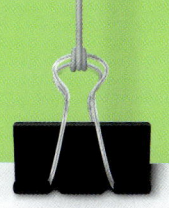

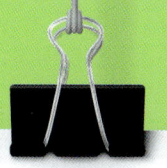

Kyla Slaven is the producer of the kids' ethics podcast *Short & Curly*. Kyla has been making radio and podcasts for a long time – working in community radio, as a reporter for triple j and heading up the then-new current affairs show *Hack*. She also worked on the philosophy podcast (for grown-ups) *The Philosopher's Zone*, where a chance encounter with a group of kids gave her the idea for *Short & Curly*. Kyla loves that her job combines the serious with the silly, and the smart with the fun.

* * *

Short & Curly has flourished thanks to the encouragement and ongoing support from a number of smart and lovely colleagues, including Ian Walker, Jo Upham and Kellie Riordan. The Short & Curly team of Carl Smith, Molly Daniels, and of course, Matt Beard, are one of the most fun, interesting and least ego-driven groups of people I have worked with.

Outside of Short & Curly HQ, I'd like to thank my close family for being interested in ideas and how they can be applied to real life: The Slavens – Trevor, Romi, Margo, Dana. Also, Dianne Blazley, Evan Lee, Janine Leake and Patrick Nielsen. Special thanks also to friends who've been a great support, including Cath Dwyer, Jason Harty, Ben Oquist, Judith Pini, Fiona Katauskas, Tim O'Connor, Laura Bloom and Brigit Berger.

Of course, some of the most important people in this whole project are the schoolchildren who have responded to my tricky and difficult questions with enthusiasm and thoughtfulness – they are always a joy to get to know. Finally, my most special thanks to my daughter, Mika, for being a kind, curious and delightful human, full of humour and optimism, and for letting me use her voice for the show when asked!

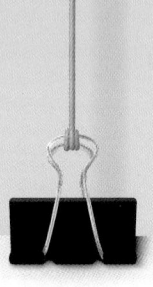

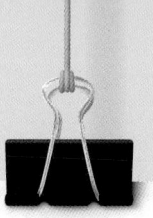

Simon Greiner is an illustrator who lives in Sydney, Australia, with his beautiful wife and two boys. His work has appeared all over the place, including the front cover of the *New Yorker* magazine, as well as in the kids' book *Regal Beagle*.